Spring Time

**My Amazing Journey from
High School Benchwarmer to
the Big Leagues to Mentor of
Major League All-Stars**

Compete w Confidence

by *Steve Springer*
with Mike Yorkey

© Copyright 2016 by Steve Springer

ISBN 13: 978-0-9981687-3-9

eBook Editions:
Adobe Digital Edition 978-0-9981687-4-6 (.epub)
Kindle and MobiPocket Edition 978-0-9981687-5-3 (.prc)

Published by Turning Page Books

Editorial assistance by Gary Springer, Ross Mitchell, Heidi Moss, Jim Yorkey, and Nicole Yorkey

Cover and interior design by Blue Muse Studio (www.bluemusestudio.com)

The *Los Angeles Times* article, "Springer Is Just Treading Water in Tidewater" by Mike DiGiovanna, has the following credit line: Copyright © 1988. Los Angeles Times. Reprinted with permission.

For more information on Steve Springer or to contact him, visit his website at www.qualityatbats.com.

Contents

Part I: My Story in Baseball

=========== *Photo Insert* ===========

Part II: Hitting a Baseball

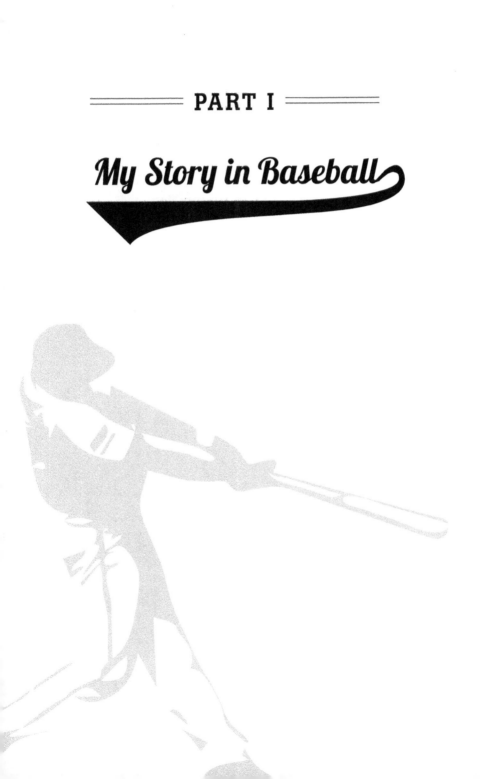

PART I

My Story in Baseball

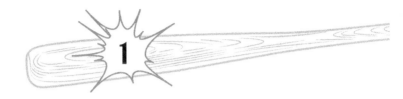

Leading Off

Springtime in the Rockies.

I had never seen such crazy weather in all my years as a baseball player. I'm talking about taking batting practice with snowflakes the size of quarters falling onto the ball field, only to evaporate once they hit the grass or infield dirt. Night games with fans wrapped in blankets to ward off the 39-degree chill. Playing the following night in temperatures so balmy that kids chased foul balls in T-shirts. Coloradans joked about having a four-season climate—all in the same day.

The unpredictable weather happened in the spring of 1990 when I was playing for the Colorado Springs Sky Sox, the Triple-A affiliate of the Cleveland Indians. I was twenty-nine years old, starting my ninth season in the minor leagues—and my sixth in Triple-A ball, one rung down from the major leagues.

So close but yet so far from The Show.

I remember chatting up one of my coaches shortly after Opening Day that season. I'll call him Hack. (Ballplayers don't call their coaches "Coach" or "Skip" any longer. We usually go by first names or nicknames.)

Hack and I were standing around the batting cage, watching fly ball after fly ball sail a long way in the thin air before landing gently beyond the outfield fence. Nothing surprising about that: Sky Sox Stadium had the highest elevation of any professional ballpark in the United States. At 6,531 feet above sea level, hitters licked their chops every time they stepped into the batter's box. The ball, it was said, carried all the way to Kansas.

Hack broke my train of thought with a startling question. "Springer, why don't you quit? You're never getting out of Triple-A. You've got a label."

Hack was one of those coaches who didn't have a filter. But he had a point. Maybe I *was* labeled as a Triple-A guy. After getting drafted by the New York Mets following my junior year of college, I had been bouncing around the minor leagues for eight long years. What Hack didn't know was how many times I'd been told I wasn't good enough from the time I was in high school until now—one step away from the big leagues. Although Hack thought I should shut it down, he obviously didn't know what was inside my heart and mind.

I thought back to the closest time I came to being called up to the major leagues. It happened in 1987—three years earlier—when I was playing second and third base for the Tidewater Tides, the Triple-A team for the New York Mets. The Tidewater Tides played their games in Norfolk, Virginia, and were part of the International League.

When news swept through the locker room that the New York Mets' second baseman, Tim Teufel, got hurt and couldn't play, a shock wave ricocheted through my nervous system. This was my chance. The guy ahead of me was injured. The Mets needed another infielder, and I was next in line. I certainly deserved a shot: I was knocking the cover off the ball, batting over .300, and showing a decent glove in the infield.

Instead of being told to pack my bags for New York, however, another infielder got the call—Keith Miller. Though I was happy for Keith, a great guy and good friend, I didn't understand the Mets' thinking. Keith was hitting .230, more than 70 points behind me, yet he was the player getting a taste of the Big Apple. Perhaps the Mets gave him a shot because he was a couple of years younger than me and wanted to see what he could do.

Keith hustled to make a flight and was in the Mets lineup that night. We were on the road at the time, so I watched the Mets game in my hotel room, extremely interested in every move Keith made. He was running from first to third on a single to the outfield when he slid into third base headfirst. It was a bang-bang play, and once the dust had settled, Keith hopped up, holding his right hand and crying out in pain. He had obviously jammed one of the fingers during the slide.

The Mets' trainer ran out to have a look, and the next thing I knew, Keith was being led off the field while a pinch runner took his place.

I called Mike Cubbage, my manager, in his room. He knew immediately why I was on the horn.

"Spring, you never know," he said. "This might be your shot if he can't play."

I set the hotel phone back down on the hook, hoping the next time the phone rang, I would be a changed man. Hoping that I would be Steve Springer, major league baseball player. My dream of making it to the big leagues—something I wanted more than anything else in my whole life—would become a reality.

I watched the rest of the game for an update on Keith's injury, thinking that bad news for him would be good news for me. The broadcasting team didn't pass along any injury reports during the rest of the game, however.

I decided to get some sleep. I tossed and turned, unable to contain my excitement. Suddenly, just after midnight, a loud ring from the bedside phone startled me. This was it. I knew, just knew, that someone in the Mets organization was on the other end of the line, ready to inform me that I was going to the big leagues.

I picked up the phone, but the voice I heard wasn't someone from the Mets' front office. Instead, it was Andre David, a left-handed hitting outfielder on our team.

"What time does the bus leave in the morning?" he asked.

Of all the questions . . . "Dude, you're calling me after midnight to ask when the bus leaves? Check the friggin' board!"

"Whoa, mellow out," he said. "I'm sorry.

I took a deep breath. "The bus leaves at ten."

The phone didn't ring the rest of the night. The next morning, Mike Cubbage told me that Keith Miller's X-rays were negative. It turned out he had dislocated his right index finger.

"So what does that mean?" I asked. Sometimes players can stay in the lineup with a dislocated finger.

"I heard he's going to tape it up and keep playing," Mike said.

And that's exactly what happened. Keith bound together his index and middle finger with adhesive tape and started the next 10 games, hitting safely in nine of them. When Tim Teufel came off the disabled list and took his place, Keith got to stay in the big leagues.

Once again, I had missed out. But I was *sooo* close to being called up. I knew I could get there, which is why I found myself in Colorado Springs in the spring of 1990, still chasing the dream.

A RAY OF SUNSHINE

I wasn't just playing for myself. I was also playing for my wife, Teri. We had been married for just three months, and she was all in with baseball. Teri was willing to go to the ends of the earth for me, and if that meant moving to Colorado Springs, then that's what she would do. She was also a great sounding board, especially in helping me keep my head screwed on straight when it came to dealing with our manager Bobby Molinaro.

Bobby didn't have a filter either. He was known around the baseball world for saying exactly what was on his mind. One time he really got on our case after a lopsided defeat. "We have some players on this team who aren't taking the game as serious as they should!" he yelled, looking around the locker room and making eye contact with each player. "All I ask is for you to stay on top of the game mentally for the two-and-a-half hours you're between the white lines. You're not doing that with any consistency. You're not developing mentally. Listen, baseball is your life! You have to dig down deeper! With the team we have, we should be five games over .500, but we're not. How much fun can we have when we're losing?"

These type of rah-rah speeches usually didn't go over very well in the clubhouse. Baseball is a long, hard grind that begins in early April and doesn't end until the end of August—at least in the minor leagues. And that doesn't include the playoffs. Although we didn't play 162 regular season games like they do in the major leagues, we still played 142 games with fewer days off. Sure, we were losing more games than we were winning, but we were still playing hard. Things just weren't clicking yet.

About six weeks into the 1990 season, John Hart, the Director of Baseball Operations for the Indians, visited the club from the front office in Cleveland. Every player knew this was a chance to make a good impression.

Once again, I was hanging around the batting cage during batting practice. When I thought no one could overhear me, I asked him the same question I asked Hack: "Hey, John. You think I've got a chance to get up there this year?"

John scratched the dirt with his black leather shoe. "Keep playing, Spring. You're doing fine." His warm and fatherly tone of voice told me this: *Stay the course, young man. You never know.*

On May 14, 1990, we were home for a three-game series against the Tucson Toros, the Triple-A affiliate for the Houston Astros. I hit a two-run home run in my first at-bat, which is always a great way to start a game. I wasn't a long ball hitter, but I had good pop in my bat, especially for an infielder.

Our lead was short-lived, however, and we were in our last at-bat in the bottom of the ninth. I came up with the bases loaded. A chance to be a hero.

I chased two sliders in the dirt, putting me in the hole with an 0-2 count. Mad at myself for swinging at bad pitches, I stepped out of the box. After taking a moment to compose myself, I stepped back in, confident and ready for the task at hand.

"Time ump!"

The call to stop the game came from our bench. The next thing I knew, I saw our manager, Bobby Molinaro, directing Beau Allred to pinch-hit for me.

Molinaro's taking me out in the middle of an at-bat with the count 0-2? What manager does that?

Beau was taking the last of his practice swings as I walked away from home plate, feeling embarrassed and humiliated. *You have to be kidding me,* I thought.

Sure, I was a right-handed hitter and Beau was a left-handed batter who would be stepping up to the plate against a right-handed reliever, but this was ridiculous. Taking me out with an 0-2 count was so bizarre that I wondered if I was on *Candid Camera*. Maybe a secret film crew was waiting for me to destroy a urinal with my bat.

Instead of retreating to the clubhouse and taking out my frustrations on some porcelain, I angrily chucked my bat toward the end of the bench and sat down to watch Beau finish my at-bat. First pitch, and he lined a base hit, scoring two runs and giving us a walk-off victory—and making Bobby Molinaro look like a managerial genius. Now I had to act like I was happy as my teammates rushed to home plate to celebrate the come-from-behind win. But I wasn't a happy camper, and I'm sure it showed.

The next day, a couple of hours before the next game against the Toros, I was told that Bobby wanted to see me in his office.

He either feels bad for pinch-hitting me or he's releasing me because I threw my bat in the dugout and showed him up.

Instead of a one-on-one meeting with my team manager, there was another person sitting in the manager's office—Indians farm director Johnny Goura. Now I was really going to get a dressing down for my mini-tantrum.

After introducing me to Johnny Goura, Bobby got down to business. "You're probably ticked off that I pinch-hit for you last night," he said.

"Yeah," I conceded. "I haven't been taken out of a game since high school. Let's just say that it wasn't a great feeling for me."

"Yeah, I'd be pissed, too," Bobby said. "But that's not why we called you in today. Turns out that Johnny's got something to tell you."

What the Cleveland farm director would say next would change my life—forever.

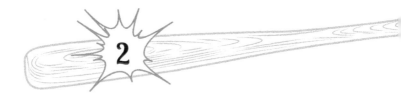

Rounding First

*G*rowing up, I got my athletic genes from my mom.

Back in the day, kids in the neighborhood called her a "tomboy," a term you don't hear much anymore. My mother, Sharon Springer, not only didn't throw a baseball like a girl, but she was an excellent fast-pitch softball player and a nationally ranked amateur bowler. She was a pretty good swimmer, too, since she grew up a few blocks from the Pacific Ocean in Seal Beach, around thirty miles southwest of downtown Los Angeles and part of Orange County.

My dad's athletic ability? Let's just say Gene Springer sucked at pretty much any sport he tried. He just wasn't as coordinated as my mom, who was a natural athlete. One of the few sports he played was golf, but he wasn't that good—a bogey golfer at best.

I remember the time when my older brother Gary and I joined him and a golfing buddy named Roger on a Saturday afternoon. We would have been in high school at the time, and Gary and I liked to mess around with the driver to see how far we could bomb the ball. Maybe we weren't the straightest off the tee, but we could airmail our drives a long way even though neither of us was that tall.

We were standing on the first tee when Dad waggled his club and poked a drive that maybe went 220 yards. Gary and I got up next, and as expected for a pair of competitive athletes, we took violent swings at the ball. When we connected well and smacked our drives a good fifty to seventy-five yards past my dad, his buddy whistled in appreciation. "There's no way these kids are yours," Roger teased my father.

My dad accepted the jibe. "They take after their mom," he smiled, and we all laughed.

Looking back through the years, I'd say that I take after both of my parents: Mom for her athletic abilities and sunny disposition while Dad gave me a determined attitude.

My father gained an appreciation for staying the course while growing up on a farm outside Hastings, Minnesota. Born in 1936, he was raised on doing farm chores. He always used to tell me how he got up at 4 a.m. to milk a dozen cows before walking four miles through snowdrifts to Hiawatha Elementary—uphill both ways.

I'm sure perching his butt on a three-legged milking stool in sub-zero temperatures shaped his character and what he became in life, which was a general contractor who supervised the construction of sheet metal buildings. The name of the company, which my father purchased after working there twenty years, was Carl Brooks, Inc. He worked long hours while I was growing up, usually leaving the house by 6:30 a.m. and not arriving home until dinnertime. He was a hard worker and great provider.

When Dad came of age back in Minnesota, he didn't want to milks cows, muck stalls, or run farm equipment through dusty fields for the rest of his life, so he enlisted in the U.S. Marines Corps upon graduating from high school. The Marines put him through boot camp at the Marine Corps Recruit Depot (MCRD) in San Diego and then stationed him forty miles north at Camp Pendleton, a Marine

Corps base along the California coast. The year was 1954, and my father was eighteen years old.

Fortunately for Dad, the Korean War was over and America was in peacetime. Even better was that my father knew how to type at a time when few guys had that skill, so he became a desk sergeant—the enlisted man who typed requisition reports all day while other Marines in his company went on 20-mile humps with 40-pound packs draped across their backs.

My father had been stationed at Camp Pendleton for a couple of years when he and a buddy got leave passes and hitchhiked to a roller rink in Santa Ana, about an hour north. I don't think they were particularly interested in strapping on a pair of ill-fitting roller skates and gingerly working their way around the rink. Roller-skating, they heard, was a good way to meet girls and have a good time.

And meet girls they did. One of them was Sharon Wakefield, an outgoing and athletic blond who could soar on skates. A year younger than my dad, she was from Seal Beach, a small beachside community wedged between Long Beach and Huntington Beach. Mom always said Seal Beach was a great place to grow up in the 1950s.

I never heard what pick-up line my dad used to gain the attention of the cute young woman from Seal Beach, but I do know that upon their introduction, Eugene Vincent Springer told his future wife that his name was "Dick Fox."

He wasn't joking. Back in those days, a lot of military knuckleheads thought they'd be better off using a pseudonym when they were on leave and painting the town red. Just in case there was trouble.

As Gene and Sharon continued seeing each other, something happened—they fell in love. *Six months* into their relationship, however, Dad was still "Dick Fox" to my mom.

Finally, he 'fessed up and told my mom his real name. There were hurt feelings, but my mom eventually got over it. I'm not so sure about her parents, though. My dad had gotten off on the wrong foot with his future in-laws when he was introduced to Lawrence and Dorothy Wakefield. Dad, in an attempt to prove that he was some kind of tough Marine guy, squeezed my grandfather's hand so hard that he fell to his knees and yelped in pain. But that was nothing compared to the betrayal his future in-laws felt when they learned "Dick Fox" was a ruse.

As they continued to date, Gene became marriage-minded. When he was twenty-four years old, he got his honorable discharge from the Marines and moved to Long Beach so he could see my mom. A born salesman, Dad started working for a construction company, selling their commercial buildings.

My dad asked my mom to marry him probably a half-dozen times. Each time she said she needed to think about it.

She finally made up her mind, and just like that, my parents decided to drive to Las Vegas, where they got married at the Little White Wedding Chapel on the Strip. The decision to elope didn't endear my father to his in-laws, as you can imagine. My mom was their only daughter, and the fact that her parents weren't able to give my mom a proper wedding was another strike against my dad.

FOUR KIDS IN FOUR YEARS

Gene and Sharon moved into an apartment in Long Beach and started their married life together. Their first child, Gary, arrived on December 23, 1959. I came along fourteen months later on February 11, 1961, followed by two sisters: Susan was born September 24, 1962, and Robin arrived on October 28, 1963.

You read that right—four kids in four years. The way things worked out we were all one year behind each other in school, which is another way of saying that my parents had *four* kids in high school at the same time.

But I'm getting ahead of myself.

In our preschool years, we moved to 6251 Mar Vista Drive in Huntington Beach. Back in the early '60s, housing tracts were sprouting up everywhere in Orange County. Times were good, and the economy was booming. My parents purchased a 1,600-square-foot rancher with three bedrooms and a den for $19,900 and wondered how they would ever make the mortgage payment each month.

Shortly after we moved in, my mom's world was rocked when her father died of lung cancer. He was young—just fifty-three. Lawrence Wakefield was a wall-and-ceiling plasterer at a time when nobody knew what asbestos was. The importance of wearing a mask wasn't known.

Mom was devastated to lose her father at such a young age. At the time of his death, Grandpa Wakefield owned a bait shop on Pacific Coast Highway about five blocks from the Seal Beach Pier. I've always said that if my grandfather had lived longer, there was a good chance that I would have become a fisherman instead of a baseball player.

But I have to credit Grandpa Wakefield with teaching me how to swing a baseball bat for the first time. A few months before his death—I was four or five at the time—he used his fishing-knot skills to tie a piece of fishing line to a tennis ball and suspend the ball from his backyard clothesline. Then he showed me how to hold a bat and smack the ball. That's how I started swinging a baseball bat. I loved hitting that tennis ball over and over.

One way Grandma Wakefield dealt with her grief following my grandfather's death was by telling my mom that she'd watch Gary and me when my parents wanted a break or traveled to weekend bowling tournaments. Grandma Wakefield didn't have the energy to watch *four* kids in her Seal Beach home, so Grandma Kiefer—my mom's grandmother, and our great-grandmother, who also lived in Seal Beach—agreed to look after my younger sisters, Susan and Robin, whenever my parents went out of town. We stayed many weekends with our Grandma Wakefield, eating poached eggs for breakfast and hitting the tennis ball on the string in the backyard all day long.

Mom was such a good bowler that she had aspirations of turning professional before she married Dad. Once kids came along, however, she had to put those dreams aside. She still liked to bowl in local and regional tournaments, which Dad supported. He did his best to pick up the game so he could bowl with her in leagues and competitions. Despite his lack of natural athleticism, he actually became a pretty good bowler who averaged in the 170s.

When we weren't in Seal Beach, our world revolved around the neighborhood on Mar Vista Drive. Every day we played with the Martin and Blaty boys who lived on Penfield Circle, a cul-de-sac that started opposite our front door on Mar Vista. Tim Martin was Gary's age, and Mark Martin was my age. The Blatys had *twelve* kids packed into their three-bedroom home—can you imagine that happening these days?—with two boys our age: Tom was Gary's age and Matt was in my class.

We were inseparable during the elementary school years. If we weren't playing over-the-line baseball at the end of the Penfield Circle cul-de-sac—using a wooden bat and a tennis ball—then we were messing around with touch football or shooting baskets at Ada Clegg Elementary and Helen Stacey Middle School, located around the corner from our home.

Most of the time, though, we played over-the-line because we loved baseball. It was either two-on-two or three-on-three—the older boys against the younger boys. We painted a "home plate" on the pavement of Penfield Circle and hit toward the end of the cul-de-sac, which was outlined by a five-foot-high sandstone masonry wall. Hit the ball over the wall, and you had a home run. But you had to climb over the wall and retrieve the tennis ball.

Here's how Mark Martin described those carefree days:

MARK MARTIN: I don't have a memory without a Springer in it. Steve and I started kindergarten together with Mrs. Powers and were best friends until third grade. That's when my parents held me back a grade because I was so small. Then the Blatys moved in, and Matt Blaty became Steve's best friend.

Steve was a natural character and very popular in elementary school, this blond-headed kid who was good-looking as well as an athlete. It doesn't come any better than that.

We played baseball every day, or so it seemed, in our front yard or out in the street. Always with tennis balls. We would get three outs, and then the other team would bat. We'd argue about what was a hit or what was an out. We would play until we got tired or hungry, and then we'd go home and get something to eat. Then we'd go play until the streetlights came on.

Steve was also my protector. There was a kid named Robbie Neibacher who always wanted to beat the crap out of me. Steve told him that he better not touch me or he was going to pound him. He was a true friend.

One time, there was going to be a "fight" between Steve and Mike O'Brien. I've long forgotten why they decided to duke it out. With a lot of excitement in the air, they met a block away on Quill Circle in front of the Staubs' house.

They were squaring off, circling each other, but no one was throwing a punch. Finally, Steve stopped and turned to me. "Mark, will you buy me 25 pieces of licorice if I slug him?"

"Sure," I said.

Just as Steve took a step toward Mike O'Brien, Mrs. Staub came running out of the house and broke things up. No blows were thrown, but that story goes to show you that Steve was the straw that mixes the drink in our neighborhood.

Besides playing over-the-line a lot, we were always figuring out new ways to have fun. One game we liked to play was "Ding Dong, Ditch 'Em." That's where we'd creep up to a house, press the doorbell, and run like hell to safe cover. Of course, we thought it was the funniest thing whenever a tubby woman in curlers or some fat balding guy in a bathrobe answered the door only to see no one there.

One of those crabby old men was Mr. Grump—not his real name, of course—who lived in the last house on Penfield Circle. For months, he'd been our favorite target. We must have rang his doorbell three times and he'd never been able to catch us. On this occasion, we tiptoed to his front door and were just about to press the—

Suddenly, the door swung open. Mr. Grump was standing there like he knew we were coming. We immediately took off, but Mr. Grump horse-collared me and twisted my right arm behind my back.

"I caught you!" he said with the wildest grin on his face.

Mr. Grump frog-marched me across the street to Tim Martin's house and made a beeline for the garden hose. Then he proceeded to douse me with a stream of water as all my friends laughed their heads off.

A safer thing to do was ride our bikes to the tomato fields at the end of Mar Vista. More often than not, the temptation of throwing ripe tomatoes at each other proved to be too great. I had a great arm and loved the *splat* each time I nailed Gary or one of my buddies.

Then the tomato fields were plowed under to make way for the Westminster Mall, one of the first enclosed shopping malls in the region. Suddenly, a big red May Company sign atop a two-level, fortress-like building dominated the landscape, but we saw the mall as a new place to get into mischief and chase the cutest girls.

You know how up-and-down escalators are separated by a long slide with bumps every yard or so to discourage kids from "escalator surfing" today? Well, those escalator bumps weren't there when the Westminster Mall opened, so we slid down those slippery chutes and landed in a heap at the bottom of the escalator—laughing the entire time.

Of course, we could get hurt but kids don't think about that when pulling stupid stunts. Thankfully, before any of us broke any bones, bumps were put in the slides to keep us from sliding down on our butts. We proudly believe the bumps were invented because of us.

Another thing we liked to do at the mall was pack into the elevator at Sears and stop it by prying open the doors between the floors. We thought it was funny to hear an old lady—who'd be waiting for the elevator to arrive on her floor above us—saying out loud, "I keep pushing the button and it's not coming. How come the elevator isn't coming?"

And then we'd yell out, "Help, help, we're stuck!"

Of course, we weren't stuck. All we had to do was allow the doors to close and the elevator would start moving again, which is what we did after an appropriate amount of time passed by. We hoped we would get a free ice cream after we "freed" ourselves, but that never happened.

That's the type of kids we were—always trying to prank somebody. We could be little brats too, especially with our sisters when we had a babysitter and Mom and Dad were bowling on a Saturday night with their friends.

Fortunately for us, my parents usually asked a teenage boy in the neighborhood, Mike Dapello, to babysit us. That was a joke; Mike let Gary and me do whatever we wanted—like bossing our younger sisters around. Actually, we made Susan and Robin do whatever we wanted.

Let's say that we were all watching *The Brady Bunch* from the living room couch but wanted to turn the channel to the Dodgers game during the commercials. There was no remote control in those days: someone had to get off the couch, walk over to the TV, and turn the knob channel by channel until he or she arrived at the right show or program. (Luckily there were only a dozen or so channels in those days.) Our remote control was called "Susan and Robin," and if they didn't turn the TV channel when Gary and I wanted, then they knew they would feel our wrath.

"Turn the channel to the Dodgers game," Gary would bark out to our sisters. As the oldest, Gary felt he had that right.

"No, you turn it," Susan would reply.

"No, you turn it," Gary would respond.

"No, you turn it," Susan volleyed.

Robin nodded in agreement. "You turn it," she said.

Now they were asking for it.

Gary would make eye contact with me; that was our cue. Then we'd rush our sisters and wrestle them until one of them agreed to turn the channel. Of course, they fussed and screamed, especially after we administered "Indian burns" by placing our hands on one of their arms and twisting it with a wringing motion to produce a burning sensation. It was either that or "Chinese torture"—using the knuckle on our index finger and thumping it on the victim's chest bone . . . over and over and over. If that didn't get Susan and

Robin to turn the channel, one of us would sit on one of our sisters and let one go.

And our babysitter Mike Dapello would be laughing his head off.

When we tired of the game, we let our sisters go, and we always knew what was going to happen next: Susan and Robin would run to the master bedroom, where our second phone was located, and try to call our parents at the bowling alley to get us into trouble.

Gary had a solution for that too—taking the phone in kitchen off the hook. That way Susan and Robin couldn't call out.

And then Gary and I would enjoy the last laugh. We were partners in pranks and teammates in baseball. We were as close as brothers could be, and it was because of our love for baseball—from Little League into college.

3

Stepping into the Bucket

*L*ife is about competing.

I can't remember if Mom voiced those words, but she didn't have to. She was always coming up with little games that pitted the kids against each other. She liked creating competition.

Take our backyard pool, for example. Dad had a swimming pool put in when I was in the fourth grade, which was a big deal because that made us the first family in the neighborhood to get an in-the-ground concrete pool. Our pool was big—probably 12-by-35 feet with a deep end that was 12-feet deep. During the hot summer months, we loved having the Martin boys and the Blaty kids over for swim parties, which is why 6251 Mar Vista became the hangout home on the block.

When the phone rang and Mom went inside to answer, that was our chance to climb onto the roof and jump into the deep end. Mom didn't think that was the safest thing to do, so one afternoon she strung a long piece of yellow rope across the pool, from the house to the backyard fence.

"Let's see how high you boys can jump off the diving board," she announced. Then we lined up and tried to jump high enough to clear the rope. Sometimes we made it, and sometimes we fell short. Those who were successful got to jump in the next "round" as Mom moved the rope a little higher. Gary always won these contests, which frustrated the rest of us.

Mom was always the organizer of games like seeing who could generate the biggest cannonball splash, best back-flip dive, or swim the most laps underwater while holding our breath. Gary usually won those contests, too. Another game she liked was to throw a handful of pennies into the pool and let us dive after them. Whoever collected the most pennies won, and sometimes I grabbed more than Gary. Win or lose, I'd beg my mom to throw the pennies back into the pool so we could dive for them all over again.

It wasn't often that I beat Gary in anything because he was always a little bigger, a little faster, and a little better than me. Then again, he was fourteen months older, but that didn't stop me from trying to beat my big brother in whatever game, contest, sport, or activity we were doing. But if there was one constant about our childhood together, it was that my big brother always had to win:

> GARY: If I didn't win, I was the biggest sore loser ever. If I had to cheat to win or improve my odds, that's what I did. Whenever we played Monopoly growing up, I had to be the banker. That way I could count out more money for myself. If we were playing cards at the dining room table, I made sure I sat opposite the big mirror on the wall so I could sneak a peak at Steve's or my sister's cards. When we ran foot races in the street, I always took off just a tad sooner than everyone else.

One way Gary tilted the odds whenever we played over-the-line was making sure he had the older kids on his team. But even if he chose the younger Martin and Blaty kids, Gary would probably win because his great hand-eye coordination and quick hands made him one of the best baseball players around. He really shined on the Little League field, where he was an All-Star shortstop, a league-leader in hitting, and one of the best pitchers. Try as I might, I could never quite keep up with Gary, much like how Wile E. Coyote could never catch the Road Runner in Saturday morning cartoons. Talk about frustrating.

My first chance to play with Gary instead of against him happened in Little League when I was nine years old. After my first season as an eight-year-old in the Farm Division, I was supposed to move up to the Minor Division as a nine-year-old, but I skipped that league and went straight to the Major Division, which was generally comprised of boys between the ages of ten and twelve. Very few nine-year-old kids got to play in the Major Division, but an exception was made for me because I was a good player for my age. I'm sure the fact that my dad was the team manager also had a lot to do with him drafting me to play alongside Gary.

Even though I was an immature third-grader playing against sixth-graders about to become teenagers, I still got to play since one of Little League's rules is that every player has to get in the game for at least two innings. Then again, I wasn't the crummiest player on the team, not by a long shot. I was probably the fifth best player, so I got my at-bats.

One of those at-bats was against Joel Willett, a flame-throwing twelve-year-old pitcher who was head-and-shoulders bigger than me. (He was also rumored to be shaving.)

Joel could rear back and throw blazing fastballs. Speed guns weren't around back then, but I'm sure Joel threw 100 mph. Then again, only 46 feet separated him from the pitching rubber to the front edge of home plate, so it didn't take long for the ball to reach the plate from the pitcher's mound.

Nobody wanted to face him. Little League games were six innings, so there was always a chance he'd strike out all 18 batters.

One time I stepped into the batter's box to face Mighty Joel Willett. I don't think I'd ever been that scared in my life. On his first pitch, he went into a long wind-up and threw the ball as hard as he could. In a split-second, I knew his fastball was going to hit me—and it was going to hurt. I managed to turn a bit before the ball hit me square in the back.

I fell to the ground in a heap; the wind got knocked out of me. Dad came running out from the dugout.

"Steve, are you okay?" he asked, as he helped me to my feet.

"I'm fine, Dad." I brushed the dirt off my uniform, but the pain was nearly unbearable. After catching my breath, I jogged toward first to take my base.

After the game, my parents took us to McDonald's. (More on eating at the No. 1 fast food chain later.)

"I'm so proud of you," Mom said between bites of french fries. "You didn't cry."

"That's because I couldn't breathe, Mom."

"Well, you just got the wind knocked out of you, that's all," she said. "You're one tough ballplayer."

Hearing that made me feel better. But I was still scared of getting hit.

About two weeks later, we faced Joel Willett and his lightning fastball again. He had a no-hitter going into the sixth and final inning. I was hoping that I didn't have to bat, but I was second in the order. I had to face him.

When it was my turn to hit—I batted right-handed—I kept reminding myself not to get drilled. That was my biggest fear. First pitch—and I bailed, meaning that instead of striding toward the pitcher with my front foot, I practically stepped out of the batter's box toward third base.

"Steve, you stepped into the bucket," my dad said from the dugout. "C'mon, now. You can hit him! Step into the ball and swing the bat!"

I gulped. I didn't want to be anywhere near the plate when that fastball came burning in there. Joel went into his wind-up and released his next pitch. I still stepped into the bucket, but not as much. I also took a big cut and smacked a line-drive double into right-center to break up his no-hitter. Standing on second base, I never felt better as I soaked up the wild cheers from my mom and other team parents in the grandstands. I was on top of the world. Not bad for a small kid who stood 4 feet, 6 inches.

The next season, I became a catcher. I had always been Gary's catcher when he wanted to practice his pitching, so I was used to squatting and trapping each pitch with an oversized mitt. Dad also wanted me behind the plate when my brother pitched because I was pretty good at catching his fastballs and curves, even the ones in the dirt, which kept the other team from stealing. (There are no lead-offs in Little League baseball.)

If someone tried to steal second, I could throw him out. I had a good arm for someone my size. Dad's experiment worked: I proved to be a good catcher, even though the bulky catcher's equipment— heavy mask, a chest protector that ran from my shoulders to my knees, and protective leg guards—threatened to swallow me up. Nonetheless, I concentrated on giving Gary a good target.

The following year, when I was eleven, Gary was twelve and probably the best player in the league. I wasn't too far behind him, though, which is why I made the All-Star team as an eleven-year-old. Not too many fifth-graders can do that. Like every kid who plays on an All-Star team, I had dreams of playing in the Little League World Series in Williamsport, Pennsylvania.

We didn't get there, but what I do remember is coming up against a Joel Willet-type pitcher in the All-Star Regionals. I struck out during my first at-bat and was totally overmatched. As I trudged back to the dugout, head down, I told my dad, who was the All-Star manager, "I can't hit this guy."

Dad wasn't going to accept that attitude. "Next time you face him, get up there and get a hit! Think positively!"

I didn't see how that was possible. He was too fast. On my next at-bat, I figured my best chance to get on base was to bunt my way on. Two blazing fastballs, and two times I failed to put the bunt down. Now I was down 0-2 in the count.

I had to swing. I put my bat back on my shoulder and then took a couple of practice cuts. I stepped back into the batter's box and watched the wind-up and delivery. As the pitch came toward me, I lunged at the ball. To my everlasting surprise, I hit a bomb that struck the flagpole in dead center. Home run!

As I rounded the bases, I heard crazy cheers from our side. My home run didn't win the game, but I sure felt good about myself.

I loved baseball. All I wanted to do was play this great game.

FAMILY LIFE

The Little League years were really fun. My mom's brother, Uncle Gary, worked at Disneyland, where he was in charge of Frontierland. Since he had such a good position, we would get free admission to the Happiest Place on Earth any time we wanted.

We were also the Griswold family long before *National Lampoon's Vacation* came out. Instead of piling the kids into the station wagon for a trip to Walley World, we drove in the reverse direction from nearby Disneyland to the Land of 10,000 Lakes—Hastings, Minnesota, where my dad was from. I don't know how my parents got all six of us into the Dodge station wagon plus all of our luggage, but we somehow managed to drive 1,931 miles over three days without the kids killing each other. We were jealous of Gary because he always got to sit in the front seat since he got carsick. My sisters and I thought he was faking it so he wouldn't have to sit in the back seat.

That was how we spent our summer vacations, which led right into the start of a new school year. We had a routine: eating cold cereal and doughnuts for breakfast, walking to school, watching the clock move so slowly until the final bell, playing baseball before dinner, eating supper, and watching some TV before we went to bed. Homework? Not so important.

Mom fed us, but she wasn't into cooking. Plus, we were a finicky family who wasn't big into vegetables, so she stuck to the basics: hamburgers, hot dogs, and the occasional casserole. There wasn't much variety at our dinner table.

One time Mom prepared tacos and Spanish rice. The tacos were okay, but the Spanish rice was a non-starter with the four kids. We weren't bashful about saying what we really thought about her Spanish rice:

"This is awful."

"Yuck, Mom."

"Do we have to eat this?"

Mom was ticked that we didn't like her cooking. Dad was still at work, so she said, "No one is leaving this table until your dad comes home."

So we sat there—the Spanish rice getting terribly cold—until Dad arrived. The four of us didn't say a thing as he sat down and waited for Mom to dish up dinner for him.

She returned a minute later and set a plate with two tacos and a generous helping of steaming Spanish rice before him. Dad took one bite of the seasoned rice, looked at her, and then looked at us. "I'm not eating this crap," he said, pointing to the Spanish rice.

Hearing Dad say that made him a hero in our eyes. Mom was miffed, however, and copped an attitude. "Okay, be that way. Forget about me ever cooking again."

After that, we ate at the McDonald's on the corner of Edwards and Edinger every night. Well, maybe not *every* night, but I bet we consumed Mickey D's four or five times a week from the time I was eight or nine until I graduated from high school—more than any family in the history of the world. I'm exaggerating, but if you figure that we ate at least four times a week at McDonald's for fifty weeks a year, times ten years, that's two thousand times. And on two thousand occasions, I ordered the same thing: two hamburgers, no pickles, no onions, fries, and an orange drink.

These days, some parents may think that taking your kids to McDonald's every night is something akin to child abuse. Or that Mom was grooming us to become like Morgan Spurlock, the guy who ate three McDonald's meals a day for an entire month but barely lived to tell about that gut-damaging experience in the 2004 movie *Super Size Me*.

Are you kidding? We loved it. We *wanted* to go to the Golden Arches. And as we got into the high school years, McDonald's became really convenient because Mom was super busy picking us up from various practices: Gary became a three-sport athlete at Marina High; Susan was really into gymnastics, practicing at a private gym three nights a week and would earn a full-ride scholarship to Long Beach State; Robin was a cheerleader who practiced every day; and I played baseball in the spring.

Mom didn't abandon cooking entirely. On the one or two nights a week she cooked, she liked making a one-dish meal with some type of meat—usually a roast—with potatoes and corn. Other go-to recipes were meatballs and mashed potatoes with French onion soup, or spaghetti, which couldn't be spicy.

Man, we were picky eaters.

NEXT STEPS

*M*y last year in Little League as a twelve-year-old went well, too, although it felt funny to be playing without Gary. The comment I heard the most was that I was a "good little ballplayer," but that didn't seem like high praise. What I noticed is that my friends were starting to grow—and I wasn't. I was the smallest kid on my Little League team as well as in my class—just 4 feet, 6 inches.

Even girls towered over me in sixth grade. This was a time when girls stopped having cooties and started catching my eye, but since most girls were a head taller than me, I was locked in as "friend zone" material, not tall enough to be considered as a "boyfriend." The girls were more mature than me in every way.

No wonder I hated going to school. Not only did I feel undersized, but I was mentally underdeveloped as well. I was a terrible reader and couldn't comprehend anything. Here's a written report that my mom and dad received at their parent-teacher conference when I was in sixth grade:

- On reading: "Very poor reading habits. Has done very poor on understanding because he won't take the time."

- On math: "Steve is extremely careless in math. He doesn't listen to instructions, so it takes him longer to understand new concepts. Needs to work on accuracy instead of speed."

- On social studies: "Steve needs to slow down when taking a test and also when doing regular assignments."

- On spelling: "Spelling is not a natural subject for Steve, and he needs to work at it a little more."

Okay, so I wasn't a great student. Einstein wasn't in my family tree. This would explain why—in the sixth grade—I didn't know what puberty was or even how to spell the word.

All I knew was two things: I loved baseball . . . and my friends were growing faster than me, which automatically made them bigger and stronger.

And there didn't seem to be anything I could do about it.

Middle Innings

*T*hey did middle school or junior high differently in the Westminster School District.

Instead of middle school being the sixth, seventh, and eighth grade, or junior high being seventh, eighth, and ninth grades, Stacey Middle School—an infield fly away from Clegg Elementary—was just seventh and eighth grade.

In place of recess, I had to take a P.E. class, which I didn't look forward to at all. That's because I had to shower before going back to my regular classes. Most of the time, if a coach wasn't looking, I would put on my regular clothes and sneak out of the locker room. If I absolutely had to shower, then I would drape a towel around my waist and take the fastest shower ever. Five seconds was long enough, right?

I couldn't help but notice that some of my friends were getting hair on their bodies. I didn't have any hair.

I was 4 feet, 8 inches tall at the start of seventh grade. I'll tell you how small I was: if I, as a seventh-grader, were able to time travel and stand next to Simone Biles, the pixie gymnast who won three gold medals at the 2016 Summer Olympics in Rio de Janeiro, I would have been looking *up* to her. She's 4 feet, 9 inches.

Fortunately, I didn't get teased about my lack of height. Everyone liked me. I was one of the cool kids, probably because I was fun to be around but also because I was Gary Springer's younger brother. He was the best baseball player, the best basketball player, and the best athlete around. And he knew he was good—because all the adults told him that. He wrote "Gary the Great" on his glove, and he was serious.

But Gary always had my back. He was the first one to protect me. As much as Gary and I fought each other and got on each other's nerves back home, he wouldn't let anyone touch me in the schoolyard. I didn't get into many fights because of him.

I looked up to my brother, and even though it seemed like I was always a step behind him on the athletic field, I knew that if I could play baseball as well as Gary, then I would be a pretty good player . . . and he wasn't *that* much better than me. But the gap was increasing between us because he was growing and I wasn't.

We differed in other ways as well. In fact, we were the living examples of the *Odd Couple*, a popular Broadway play and feature film in the late 1960s as well as a hit TV sitcom in the early '70s. Gary was the fastidiously clean Felix Unger (played by Jack Lemmon in the Hollywood movie), and I was the slovenly Oscar Madison (played by Walter Matthau). This is how Gary described things:

> GARY: I was a neat freak, and Steve was a slob. There's no other way to put it. Steve was an absolute sluggard who left his clothes, books, and stuff everywhere. Things got so bad in the bedroom we shared that I put tape on the floor across the middle of the room. One side was mine, and the other side was his. He could put his stuff anywhere he wanted . . .

as long as it stayed on his side of the tape.

We would get into arguments and wrestling matches about him putting his stuff on my side of the room. One summer we collected Dairy Queen ice cream cups that were shaped like baseball helmets and included the logos of major league teams. The idea is that after you finished your ice cream, you kept your helmet as a memento and could collect all the National and American League teams.

I would put a thumbtack through the back of each plastic helmet and pin them up on my wall, putting every single team helmet two inches apart, lined up just right. But for Steve, his Dairy Queen helmets were everywhere—on the carpet, on his bed, on the dresser we shared. Some were on the wall hung haphazardly with no rhyme or reason. Really sloppy. He drove me crazy!

Here's another example: I made my bed like my Marine father would—you could bounce a quarter off the top blanket. If Steve tried to bounce a quarter off his bed, you'd never find the coin again. He didn't know what a clothes hamper was and never put any of his dirty clothes away. He was a messy guy.

I took after my mom, I'm afraid. She was a pack rat who wouldn't throw away anything. We were afraid to open the garage door because boxes were stacked so high that stuff would tumble into the driveway. She collected everything and anything and was known in the neighborhood as the knickknack lady. If there was a flat surface in the house—end tables, a china cabinet, or a coffee table—Mom made sure she filled it with commemorative plates, bowling trophies, gymnastic medals, wooden animals, and Currier & Ives snow globes. She loved going to swap meets and buying trinkets.

We didn't have any blank walls in our home either. There were pictures from family vacations, bowling tournaments, old-time black-and-whites of Seal Beach, and winners' ribbons as well as photos of her four children grinning for the camera from infancy through high school. The hallway to the bedrooms was School Picture Row for the four children: kindergarten, first grade, second grade, third grade . . . by the time I graduated from high school, our school portraits were an inch apart so that they would all fit. Those glossy 8-by-10s stayed on our walls for the next thirty years.

I'm not sure why Gary was a clean freak and I wasn't, but I was never taught to clean up. Here's how my youngest sister Robin remembers things:

> ROBIN: There's no doubt that the boys were put on a pedestal by my parents—Gary more so than Steve. On Saturday mornings, Susan and I had to clean the front three rooms—living room, dining room, and kitchen—before we could do anything. The boys? They only had to take out the trash. The chores were very one-sided.
>
> Not only were we their slaves when they told Susan and me to change the channel for them, but they got to do what they wanted to do, which was to play their sports. Even though Susan and I were into our sports, they got away with more stuff and didn't have to do much at all. It was really quite unfair.

Robin has a point. I was lazy around the house. My parents were softies, although my father liked to say, "My boys aren't afraid of hard work. They'll lay down right beside it every time."

His line was always good for a laugh, although there was more than a grain of truth in what he said. I didn't have to do chores because my parents didn't make Gary and me do them.

One time my father came home from work and found Matt Blaty mowing the lawn in the front yard on a warm summer late afternoon.

"Matt, what are you doing?" my dad asked.

"Well, I'm mowing your lawn because you're paying me to," Matt replied.

"What do you mean I'm paying you? I've got two able boys who can mow the lawn."

"Mrs. Springer asked me to mow the lawn, so you'll have to talk to her."

I can't remember why Gary or I didn't mow the lawn that day. I like to think it's because we had baseball practice or a weekend tournament, but we probably rode our bikes to the beach to do some body surfing.

We were always packing our summers with fun activities. Starting in middle school, we'd get to go to Disneyland *without* our parents. Gary, myself, and a handful of Martin and Blaty kids would squeeze into our blue Dodge station wagon, and Mom would drop us off at Disneyland at 9 a.m. and return at midnight. We had an absolute blast having the run of the Magic Kingdom.

Since this was back in the day when Disneyland had ticket books, we had only so many "E tickets" for the big rides (the Matterhorn Bobsleds, the Submarine Voyage, Pirates of the Caribbean, etc.). So we had to find other things to do, like going over to Snow White's Wishing Well, where we put gum on the end of straws and fished out quarters so we could buy an ice cream. Then it was off to Tom Sawyer Island, where we played a "Hide and Seek" game by hiding from each other in the caves that dotted the island.

When we were older, we pulled off the most outrageous prank. (And don't try this on your next visit folks.) One night, at 11:55 p.m., just five minutes before the midnight closing, the five of us rushed over to Pirates of the Caribbean for one more ride. The departure area was empty.

Over the years, we had gone on that ride probably a hundred times and knew every square inch of the attraction, from the talking skull and crossbones telling us that "there be plundering pirates lurkin' in ev'ry cove, waiting to board" to rousingly singing "Yo ho, yo ho, a pirate's life for me" at the top of our lungs with the soundtrack.

One of the guys—okay, I'll blame Matt—had an idea: we'd all jump out of the boat as it came upon the jail where imprisoned pirates—doing their best to escape advancing flames—held out a bone and a noose for a small dog just out of their reach. In the dog's mouth was a round key chain that would provide their escape.

For some reason, we knew the security cameras didn't cover that one spot. We jumped out, laughed our heads off, let a few empty boats pass, and then got back in new boats one by one. Now we were on five different boats.

When we got off at the end of the ride, we were greeted by someone from Security, who had noticed that the five fidgety boys in one boat were now spread out on five vessels. What was he going to do? Throw us out of the park? Disneyland was closed.

"Never do this again," he ordered in a brusque manner, and we *promised* we would never jump out of a Pirates of the Caribbean boat again.

We weren't afraid to try anything when we hit our teen years, including square dancing, a dance for four couples that begins with each couple facing one of the other couples so that the four couples form a square.

We were introduced to square dancing by Tim Martin's dad, who was a square-dance caller on weekends. One night at Tim's house, his father showed us all the basic moves, explaining that square dancers have to work as a team. I remember memorizing a large number of potential steps and learning to wait for the caller to "call" the parts of the dance. With Mr. Martin's encouragement, we tried out square dancing at a school gymnasium in Westminster and liked it—not because we wanted to dress up like cowboys but because we wanted to meet girls—and hold their hands while the dance was called.

But wasn't square dancing . . . *swing your partner 'round and 'round, turn your corner upside down* . . . for squares, especially in the early 1970s? Well, square dancing back then was a precursor for line dancing today—the difference being that square dancing is always done with a partner while in line dancing, you're generally on your own while you concentrate on making the correct steps.

Looking back, it was such innocent fun. I just wish I wasn't so immature physically and emotionally.

A BIGGER FIELD

*W*hen you're smaller than your classmates and not growing, you think about why your friends are sprouting like weeds and you're not. During my middle school years, I would have been the perfect candidate for the Vienna Boys Choir. My angelic voice wasn't cracking like my buddies in the neighborhood.

I don't remember Dad sitting me down for a "birds and the bees" talk or doing anything to prepare me for adolescence. That was fairly normal for the time, the early '70s. I did overhear them talking one time about how small I was, but nothing was ever made of it. They never took "little Stevie" to the doctor to see if there was something wrong with my pituitary gland or if there was something they could do to help me grow. In other words, seeking a medical opinion for my "short stature"—which is what the syndrome is called today—wasn't on their radar screen.

Things are much different nowadays. Currently, pediatricians measure children on the Centers for Disease Control Clinical Growth Chart and inform parents where their children stand in comparison to their peers. I would imagine that I would have been at the bottom of the chart, in the 5th percentile.

Doctors counsel parents of short stature children to pay attention to a balanced diet of protein, carbohydrates, and fats, but nutrition was an afterthought in our family. I've already described how I was raised on McDonald's hamburgers and orange soda. Milk for growing bones? I hated milk.

I did grow some during my middle school years, but my lack of development was really evident on the baseball diamond. I was a Little League All-Star catcher when I was eleven and twelve, but once I hit seventh grade and turned thirteen, I graduated to the Senior Majors, which played their baseball games on fields with the same dimensions as a major league ball field.

Base paths were 90 feet, a third longer than Little League's 60-foot distance between bases. Outfield fences were 320 feet down the lines and up to 400 feet in center field instead of 200 feet to all points of the outfield fence in Little League. A major league infield meant that throws from home plate to second base were 127 feet instead of 84 feet, the Little League distance.

A major league-sized field was too big for me. I couldn't make the throw to second base to catch anyone stealing. Dad, who was my coach again (Gary and I were reunited as teammates), moved me to second base—where the smallest guy always plays.

I don't remember much about my seventh and eighth grade years in baseball. I was still a good athlete. The hand-eye coordination was there. I could hit singles and Texas Leaguers—pop flies that fall to the ground between the infield and the outfield—but playing on a regulation baseball diamond diminished my baseball skills considerably. I couldn't compete against my peers on a bigger field.

Then our family was thrown for a loop when I was in eighth grade. Gary was a freshman at Marina High in Huntington Beach and played basketball, a winter sport. As soon as the hoop season ended, he grabbed his glove and headed to the baseball field to play on the frosh-soph team made up of freshmen and sophomore players. Here's what happened next:

GARY: Everyone on the frosh-soph team had been in a baseball class while I was playing basketball, so the coaches didn't know me. I was given a two- or three-day tryout. I thought I did awesome—and then I got cut.

I was shocked to learn that I didn't make the team. So was my family. How could I be cut when I had been on All-Star teams every year and many of the players on the frosh-soph team hadn't?

My dad and I talked about what we thought happened, and the best we could figure out was that one of the players who made the team had a mom who was a school administrator and he'd been in the baseball class all semester. I was a victim of the politics of sports. Sometimes it's who you know, not how you play, that decides who makes it and who doesn't.

I was pretty bitter about how it all went down and was angry and mad. But I used that experience to become even more resolved about playing baseball, so I signed up for Pony League that spring and played well. The next year I played on the Marina High frosh-soph team and played even better, well enough to be named the MVP.

I would find out about the politics of sports when I played in the minor leagues. That said, it's good Gary came back and played his sophomore year because he's the reason I made the frosh-soph team when I started high school. The coaches saw how good he was and figured some of his baseball talent rubbed off me. I was a liability, however, because I was still under five feet my freshman year—4 feet, 11 inches to be exact.

One time I overheard our coaches talking about me while they were going over the lineup. "The kid's too small to play," said Lonnie Clausen, the assistant coach. "I don't know where we can put him."

"Yeah, he's only on the team because of his brother," said Andy Donegan, the head coach.

The coaches were right: I was riding on Gary's coattails. Since I was the last person sitting on the bench, I volunteered to coach first base, happy to be doing something during the game. Then, in the last game of the season, I finally got inserted into the lineup against Western High in the sixth inning after we had built a 7-0 lead. I pinch-hit in the top of the sixth and flared a single to right field, so that felt really good.

I took my position at second base for a one-two-three inning in the bottom of the sixth. Then in the bottom of the seventh, still with a 7-0 lead, the Pioneers got a few hits. A couple of batters walked. Several runs scored. But all we needed were two more outs and we'd win the game.

With the bases loaded and one out, a grounder came my way at second base. I mistimed getting my glove down, and the ball skidded into short right-center field. Two more runs scored. Now we were only up 7-5 with runners on second and third and just one out.

I kicked the infield dirt in frustration. I should have fielded that ground ball—or at least knocked it down to save a run.

Suddenly I heard some commotion from our dugout. I looked

over, and Coach Donegan was talking to Sparky King, a teammate of mine, and pointing in my direction. I saw Sparky nod and start sprinting toward me.

"What are you doing?" I asked upon his arrival.

"Coach told me to take your place."

"In the middle of the inning?"

"Yeah."

That was a short leash. Just as short as my stature.

Humiliated, I fought back tears as I jogged in. Play had stopped, of course, so everyone's head swiveled and watched me take a seat at the end of the bench. Mom and Dad were in the grandstands with parents of my teammates, mortified by what they had just seen. No one gets taken out defensively in the *middle* of an inning.

I sat down on the bench and buried my face into my glove. I didn't want anyone to see me crying.

Would I ever get to play the game I loved?

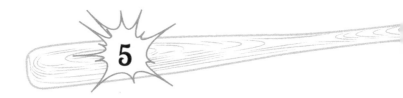

5

Into the Lineup

I grew the summer between my freshman and sophomore year at Marina High—three whole inches. Now I was up to 5 feet, 2 inches.

The rise in height secured my spot on the frosh-soph team, but my buddies were promoted to the JV team. I was fine being a starter on the frosh-soph team and ended up getting about 30 at-bats with maybe nine or 10 hits. More importantly, I was playing again instead of sitting.

I turned sixteen at the start of my sophomore baseball season. Like every kid growing up in the Southern California car culture, I really wanted my own wheels. That meant I needed to earn some money to buy my first car.

Gary had gotten a cushy job as an usher at a nearby Edwards Theater when he turned sixteen, the first year he could legally work. Mom was a film fanatic who loved going to the movies every week and had gotten to know the manager, Mr. Hammer, so she asked him to give Gary a job. When my brother told me how easy the work was—tearing tickets, pointing people to the right screening theater, and sweeping up popcorn—that sounded like a great part-time job to me. Plus, I could see all the movies I wanted for free. (In fact, I, along with my friends, never paid to see a movie for the next twenty years because my sister Susan started working at Edwards Theaters when she turned sixteen and ended up staying with Edwards for twenty years as a full-time employee.)

I had my best friend Matt Blaty get a job at the movie theater too. To help pass the time, we developed a hand signal between us. If a girl our age came through the ticket line, we gave her a thumb's up or thumb's down in a way that she wouldn't notice but Matt or I would. It was all about having fun and making the time pass quickly.

One time, Mr. Hammer called Matt and me over. The theater manager was an crabby old man who weighed 400 pounds and liked to throw his weight around, so I thought he noticed the hand-signaling going on between Matt and me. Instead, he had a request.

"I'm hungry, so I want you two to get me some food. Can you do that?"

"Sure, Mr. Hammer," I replied.

"You know the Der Wienerschnitzel up the street?"

Matt and I nodded.

"I want you to get six chili dogs and three large french fries."

Matt and I looked at each other. "We don't want anything, Mr. Hammer," Matt said.

"Yeah, we're not hungry," I chimed in.

"The hot dogs aren't for you guys! So get going!"

"Yes, sir!" Matt said.

We did our best to not burst out laughing until we cleared the front doors. *Can you imagine eating six hot dogs and three fries in one sitting!*

But there were times my adolescent appetite was so big that I would have had no trouble gobbling down a half-dozen Der

Wienerschnitzel chili dogs and all those fries. During my sophomore and junior years, my parents complained how I was eating them out of house and home—I was finally going through a growth spurt. From the time I started working at the Edwards Theaters until the start of my junior year—a period of six months—I got taller by *four* inches. I grew so rapidly that my knees hurt and would wake me up in the middle of the night.

Now I was up to 5 feet, 6 inches, which meant I had gone from "tiny" to just plain "small." Maybe I wasn't big enough to compete with the big boys on the varsity team, but I could hold my own against the sophomores and juniors who played on the JV teams in the Sunset League. I was an everyday player for the second year in a row when I started at second base my junior year. Even better, I was the best hitter on the Marina High JV team and was named Most Valuable Player at the season-ending team banquet. I can't remember what my batting average was, but it was probably in the .350 range.

It helped my cause that Coach Joe Crider believed in me—although I started noticing that if I got on base in close games after the fifth inning, he'd replace me with a pinch runner—Rich Gomez, a buddy of mine.

That bothered me. That meant I couldn't play anymore. The next time Coach Crider lifted me for a pinch runner, I asked him, "Why are you taking me out, Coach?"

"Because Rich is faster than you," he said in his syrupy Southern drawl.

"No, he isn't."

"Okay, let's have a race between you two tomorrow."

"I don't want to race!" I knew I could beat Rich. I didn't want to embarrass him.

"Then I'll keep pinch running for you."

I didn't want that either, so the following day after practice, Rich and I lined up at home plate. Coach Crider dropped his arm, and we sprinted for first base. I beat him by a full stride, and that was the last time I was taken out of a game for a pinch runner.

Meanwhile, Gary was tearing up the Sunset League in his final year of high school baseball. I saw how driven he was, but he was also a versatile athlete. His frosh-soph baseball coach, Andy Donegan, talked him into going out for the varsity football team his junior year, and he became an All-Conference wide receiver his senior year. He was a hot-shooting guard on the freshman and sophomore basketball team, but quit basketball to focus on baseball, where he really shined. Gary would be named All-League his senior year for his stellar play at shortstop and good bat, just as he was All-League his junior year.

Gary's goal was to play baseball at a four-year college, but he wasn't quite good enough—or perhaps tall enough at 5 feet, 8 inches—to get recruited by a big school. After talking through his options with Mom and Dad, he decided to enroll at Golden West College, a two-year community college a few miles from our home. Golden West had a great baseball program and was one of the top junior college teams in the state. Many players went on to star at big baseball schools like UCLA, USC, and Arizona State. They called Golden West a "feeder" school.

The summer leading up to my senior year of high school, I couldn't believe how focused Gary was on playing baseball at the college level. He got on a lifting program, which inspired me to get into weight training as well. I couldn't bench 100 pounds when I started, but I knew I needed to get stronger in the weight room, so that's where I spent a lot of time that summer.

I liked following the example set by my brother. I knew if I could keep up with him, then I'd do all right.

SENIOR STUFF

*T*ime to step up.

I had high hopes for my last year of high school baseball. I grew two more inches during the summer months to reach 5 feet, 8 inches and 140 pounds. (Gary added a final inch to his frame and stood 5 feet, 9 inches, his present height.) I had filled out my upper body, thanks to the weight-lifting program I diligently followed. I had nobody ahead of me on the depth chart. I even bought my first letterman jacket and wore it proudly.

Paul Frey was the head coach. He started me at second base, but I noticed that he kept a close eye on a sophomore named Bob Grandstaff. He was a good power hitter and was solid defensively.

I started the first four or five non-league games with a bang, hitting a home run and a few doubles. I was playing and batting well. Then in a game against Rancho Alamitos, I noticed I wasn't in the starting lineup. My heart skipped a beat. I looked at the lineup card closer. Bob Grandstaff was the new second baseman.

A horrible feeling filled the pit of my stomach. If I couldn't play second base, I didn't have many options. I could make a case to Coach Frey to try me at third base, but we already had a good third baseman, Ron Layton.

What about the outfield? I had terrible depth perception. I couldn't pick up a fly ball very well, which meant that I never got a "jump" on the ball—and that's what coaches want to see in an outfielder. Even on deep, high fly balls—the "can of corn" variety where the outfielder has plenty of time to get under the ball—I would misjudge the fly ball and watch it land five yards to either side of me. Not good. Coach Frey had seen me take outfield practice, so he knew he couldn't stick me in right field to keep my bat in the lineup.

So I sat—and watched Bob Grandstaff launch a missile over the left field wall in his very first game. When the home run sailed over the fence with plenty of room to spare, something told me that I would never play another baseball game for Marina High. Turned out I was right, which was a huge disappointment. To keep my head in the game, I returned to my old haunt—coaching first base.

College coaches don't recruit players who sit on the bench and coach first base when his team is at-bat. Even though there were fifty schools of higher learning within fifty miles of Huntington Beach, no college coach was interested in having me play for him—or even try out for his baseball team.

When my parents and their friends asked me what I wanted to do in life, I had no clue what to do about my future. Like baseball, I didn't have a lot of options there either. I was a C-minus student who brought home report cards filled with Ds in Western History, Modern U.S. History, Marine Biology, and Spanish. I couldn't even get an A as a first-period Department Aide! I got a B in that "class."

The only subject I excelled in was P.E. Mr. Polesky, who gave me an A my senior year, wrote "Great athlete, excellent attitude" on my report card. Another physical education teacher, John Seely, was a football coach who loved playing me in badminton because I was the only kid at Marina High who could beat him. He loved the competition, and so did I.

But I didn't want to play badminton in college. I wanted to play baseball. That was the game I loved, the only major sport in America contested without a time clock.

Beginning at the moment the umpire shouts, "Play ball!", I loved how baseball moved to its own distinct rhythms. The leadoff batter steps into the box, and the pitcher fidgets on the mound before hurling his first pitch—and then the game proceeds at its own pace. Throw the ball. Swing the bat. Three strikes and you're out. Four balls and take your base. Touch home plate and score a run. Nine innings make a game. The number of ways a ballgame can play out are as infinite as the stars in the heavens or the particles of sand on the seashore.

I wasn't done with my dream. I wasn't giving up. All I needed was a chance, so I went with my only option—following in Gary's footsteps and enrolling at Golden West College, a two-year school. Since Gary was considered one of the best middle infielders around— he'd won All-League honors—I was sure I'd have an in with the legendary Fred Hoover, Golden West's first baseball coach who was well-connected in the collegiate baseball world. The Springer name had to count for something with Coach Hoover.

I didn't have to wait until the fall semester to try out. The Golden West baseball team played in a summer league, so tryouts happened a week after I graduated from high school on June 15, 1979, a Friday.

I quickly learned that Coach Hoover, who'd enlisted in the U.S. Air Force in 1948 and served four years in Japan, was a no-nonsense disciplinarian but also a devoted coach who was like a second father to many of the players, including Gary. Some called him "Hoov," but there was no way that I, a freshly graduated high school player, would ever call him that. He was "Coach Hoover" to me.

The tryouts happened over a weekend. We took batting practice. We fielded ground balls. We had a big intersquad game. I got only one at-bat and struck out. Hands-down I was the smallest guy out there. To tell you the truth, I sucked.

Still, I was the brother of Gary the Great, right? Perhaps Coach Hoover could find a spot for me at the end of the bench. I had a lot of experience coaching first base.

All the players who tried out hung around the Golden West ball field—which would be named Fred Hoover Baseball Field after his retirement—waiting for the posting of a sheet containing the names of the players who made the team. Suddenly, Coach Hoover, with a military gait, appeared and tacked up the sheet to the back of the dugout. The aspiring players rushed over to have a look.

In the scrum, I couldn't see over the shoulders of my competition. As players filed away, I stepped closer to the dugout wall. My heart was in my throat. This was it.

I scanned the list. Down and then up. Down again. Up once more. My name wasn't there. I wasn't on the team. I had been cut.

My feelings were hurt, and I felt my eyes tearing up. The disappointment was huge.

I ducked out from the other players, the brim of my hat pulled low over my wet eyes. I didn't look right or left as I made a beeline for my car. All my dreams of playing college baseball evaporated that afternoon. I would never play a game of organized baseball again. This was the end of the line.

I felt pretty sorry for myself as I fought back tears. I only lived a couple of miles from the school, but that was the longest drive ever.

When I told Mom and Dad what happened, they couldn't believe I didn't make the team.

"That's too bad," Dad said.

"Yeah, quite a shame," Mom added.

There really wasn't much else to say.

My baseball career was over.

WORKING A PADDLE

There was one coach who wanted me on his team, however. That would be my uncle, Gary Wakefield, who was a big honcho at Disneyland. It seems that slow-pitch softball was a huge deal at the Magic Kingdom. There were no softball diamonds inside the Happiest Place on Earth, of course, but the Disneyland softball league—open only to employees—was a cradle of competition. Uncle Gary recruited me to play on his softball team, which was comprised of Disney supervisors who tended to be older than the average "cast member." I would be the young upstart.

But first, I needed a job at Disneyland. Uncle Gary arranged for me to become a "frontiersman" on the Davy Crockett Canoes attraction in Frontierland. I'd get to dress up in a buckskin outfit with a coonskin cap and moccasins and guide Disney guests around Rivers of America, the artificial river surrounding Tom Sawyer Island.

The canoe ride, which opened July 4, 1956, was one of Disneyland's oldest. What was unique about the canoe ride was that it was the only Disneyland attraction that was powered by park visitors—and didn't travel on a submerged track like the Mark Twain Riverboat or Sailing Ship Columbia, which toured Rivers of America as well. From their fiberglass canoe, twenty guests could see a Native American tribe (known as "Indians" back then), a "burning" cabin, and various "wildlife" that were really animated robots.

I was down with being a canoe guide. I liked being out in the fresh air, but more importantly, I liked how I got to use my arms with each paddle stroke. And there were a lot of paddle strokes, I discovered, during a full workday at the Happiest Place on Earth. I still get sore thinking about it.

At any rate, there were two canoe guides in each thirty-five-foot canoe—one at the bow and one at the stern. The guide in the lead position interacted with the park visitors the most and was responsible for instructing everyone on how to, well, row a canoe, while the guide in the back steered.

I can still remember my spiel when I was at the bow of the canoe. I started by saying, "Paddles up!"

Once everyone held his or her paddles aloft, I continued. "Welcome to the Davy Crockett Explorer Canoe Ride. This canoe will not move unless you put your paddles into the water and pull, and I don't want to be the only guy pulling. We are not on a track, so I need you to paddle. Everyone ready? Good. Off we go!"

After four trips around Tom Sawyer Island, I got a twenty-minute break. It was a great job. I loved it, and I met a lot of nice people who were invariably in good moods because they were at Disneyland, although there were some lazy dudes on the ride. The long lines reflected the popularity of this attraction.

I also met a lot of nice people playing in the Disneyland softball league, which was a pretty big deal. There were something like 7,000 Disneyland employees back then, so they must have had 150 softball teams playing for bragging rights. Plus I got to play some form of baseball, which took a bit of the sting out of getting cut.

I asked Uncle Gary if he had a job for my best friend Matt Blaty. My uncle did. Matt wanted to be a sweeper because it paid 60 cents more per hour back then. (I think I made $4.50 an hour in 1979). Sweepers were the guys dressed in ice cream white from head to toe who roamed around the amusement park picking up trash—and horse droppings—with a broom and dust pan. One of the perks was talking to cute girls and posing for pictures.

I remember the time when a cutie my age flirted with me on the canoe ride. Maybe it was the longish blond hair flowing out of my coonskin cap or the buckskin outfit, but she kept looking back and making eyes at me. This time, I was in the back steering the canoe, and she was seated directly in front of me.

It was nearing dusk, the last ride of the day. Suddenly, she dipped her paddle in the water and took a long stroke. Next thing I knew, I was on the receiving end of a big splash of water.

Did she just get me wet?

She looked back and laughed. Then she splashed me again!

"Whoa, stop please. We're about to arrive at our final destination."

One more devious look—and another splash!

By now, I was fairly soaked—and fairly teed off. I gripped my paddle tighter and—*boom, boom, boom*—drenched her for all it was worth.

I probably broke every rule in the Disney cast member handbook, but I didn't care. That is, until a lady on the canoe walked into the Guest Relations office at Disneyland City Hall on Main Street and complained about the frontiersman who splashed her daughter, getting her dress wet.

When I received a summons to visit City Hall, I felt like I was going to the principal's office. Upon walking in, I immediately recognized the gruff man seated behind the desk. It was Mr. Bailey, the centerfielder on my Disney softball team.

Mr. Bailey barely looked up from his paperwork. "Don't do that again," he growled. "You can go now."

I nearly floated out of Mr. Bailey's office, thankful I still had a job working the canoes. Then again, I had a feeling that I wouldn't get fired because we had a playoff game on Saturday and I was the starting shortstop.

And then I received even better news.

6

Digging in at the Plate

A couple of weeks after I started rowing canoes at Disneyland, I had a day off.

I didn't want to go anywhere or do anything. Maybe I felt that way because I was still bummed about being cut. Or maybe I was peopled-out. Working at a major theme park like Disneyland can do that to you.

Early in the afternoon, I was sitting with Mom on the living room couch and watching *The Young and the Restless*, a soap opera she got me hooked on. I can't remember what Jill Abbott and Katherine Chancellor were feuding about, but I'll never forget what happened next.

I heard the front door open. Standing there was Gary, who'd been at baseball practice. Golden West had started summer league, but I hadn't gone to watch him play. Too painful.

Cradled in Gary's arms were a pair of baseball uniforms. "Here," he said, tossing the pile in my direction.

I held up the jerseys for a closer look. One had an oversized G on the left side of a canary-yellow jersey. The other jersey was a gray away uniform that said **Golden West** across the chest. The numbers on the back were the same—2.

"You have a new number?" I asked. I knew that Gary had been No. 7 during his freshman year because he loved Mickey Mantle.

"No," he replied. "That's your number."

My number?

"Whaddya mean, my—?"

"You're on the team. Hoov had three guys quit."

I leaped off the couch and nearly hit the ceiling with my head. "That's awesome! Mom, can you believe this?"

My mother beamed, but then a dark thought came across my mind. "You better not be messing with me," I said to my brother.

Gary put up his hands in a defensive posture. "Dude, would I joke about something that means this much to you? You're on the team, buddy."

I didn't completely believe my brother until I joined him at practice the next day and was told by Coach Hoover to loosen up my arm. Then I played a little pepper near the backstop with the guys. I was back in baseball, the game I loved. Putting on a Golden West uniform boosted my confidence on and off the field.

Just because I made the team didn't mean I was going to play. Once again, I was the last player on the bench. Once again, I coached first base.

I never got one at-bat during summer league, but I kept working on my baseball skills. Since I wasn't taking infield with the starting team, I stationed myself at second base during batting practice and fielded balls that came my way. I made sure I took my hacks in BP, but many times I got only a few swings.

I kept my baseball skills sharp in the Disneyland slow-pitch softball league, where we made the playoffs. I was the team's best hitter, batting in the clean-up spot. I also played shortstop and anchored the infield, so I was getting in-the-game experience. It helped that Chuck Ramshaw, a Disneyland security guard who played on the USC baseball team when the Trojans won the 1968 College World Series, took me under his wing. Chuck and his wife, Shirley, would become two of my best friends for life. Uncle Gary also juggled my canoeing schedule so that I could fit everything in—my summer league games as well as being the designated ringer on the Disney softball team.

This was a happy time in my life, made more so because I had another growth spurt—at age eighteen! I grew *another* two inches that summer. I was now up to 5 feet, 10 inches, which was the average height of an American male and only two inches under the average height of major league baseball players, which was six feet. The playing field was leveling out.

After Labor Day, I enrolled at Golden West and continued to live at home. My parents let Gary move out of our bedroom and take over the den, so we each had our own room. Dad wasn't about to pay for us to get our own place, which made sense. We were always on the go. I worked the Disney canoe ride on weekends (and longer stretches over the Thanksgiving and Christmas breaks as well), enjoyed an active social life, and showed up for baseball practice every afternoon, so I was never home anyway.

Choosing my classes was interesting. I didn't have any sort of major in mind. When I looked through the syllabus, I searched for classes that fulfilled two criteria: they had to be fun and they had to be easy. That wasn't a cinch because I had to take a few "solids" to be a legitimate college student. Here's what my class schedule looked like for the fall semester of my freshman year:

- Marine Life
- Intro to Business

- Health Education
- Intro to Psychology
- Baseball Conditioning
- Baseball Sport

I lasted one month in Intro to Psychology before pulling the plug. The class material overwhelmed me with monosyllabic words and phrases like associationism, cognitive dissonance theory, empiricism, and independent variables. I took a W (for withdrawal) and concentrated on passing my other three main classes.

I managed to eke out a pair of C's in Intro to Business and Health Education, but my grade-point average took a hit with a big fat D in Marine Life. Fortunately, I had four units of A's from my two baseball classes to give me a 2.42 overall GPA.

You'd think that I would have been worried receiving such a dismal report card, but I really wasn't, and here's why: I had been receiving those type of grades all my life. Schoolwork had *always* been a challenge for me. Sure, I *wanted* to do better, but I *couldn't*. My goal was to keep skating on this sheet of thin academic ice and hope I made it to the other side—wherever that was—before the ice broke and I sank beneath the frigid waters.

It should come as no surprise that I was focused on baseball anyway. Practice started in the fall and carried right into the start of the season at the end of January. Once again I lingered on the bench when the regular season started. The rest of the time—you guessed it—I coached first base.

The Golden West Rustlers would play a lot of games—37—and would post its ninth consecutive winning season with a 24-13 record. Our best player was actually smaller than me. Even though he was just 5 feet, 6 inches, Jack Settle from Santa Fe High in Whittier led the team in hits, doubles, home runs, and RBIs while batting .366.

Then again, he was twenty-four years old, having delayed going to college to work on the railroad. He was built like a brick outhouse.

My brother Gary, our shortstop, didn't have the same build but he was right behind Jack. Gary batted a solid .340 and belted a state-leading 10 triples (and would set a school record of 15 triples in his two seasons with Golden West). My brother also established an all-time mark of 64 runs scored, as well as a record 42 walks. He was also a slick fielder who set a record for the best fielding percentage at his position.

College coaches—always on the hunt for talent—sat in the grandstands of every game, taking notes. They could see that Gary was a brilliant shortstop and swung a powerful bat for someone his size. It was evident that my brother's baseball career wasn't ending but starting in many ways.

We all knew he would be playing at a major university in the fall—and that was pretty exciting to talk about at home.

OPPORTUNITY KNOCKS

*E*ven though we had a good team and won a lot of games, that didn't earn me any innings. My best chance to play baseball was in the intersquad contests that Coach Hoover liked to organize between real games.

With a week or two to go in the season, we were holding our last intersquad game. Coach Hoover liked to coach third base for *both* teams so that he could manage the game as well as stop play and tutor the players about something that happened on the field.

I usually sat for the intersquad games, too, but on this afternoon, I got to play second base, batting ninth in the order. That was all right; at least I was playing.

Even though I was competing against my teammates, I was excited to be playing baseball. I remember taking a knee in the on-deck circle, waiting for my first at-bat. Steve Slaton, one of our best pitchers, was on the mound. I wasn't psyched out when it was my turn to hit. I strode up to the plate like I belonged there. Every batter has to bring a positive attitude to home plate.

"Time out!"

The bellowing voice came from the third base coaching box. It was Coach Hoover, motioning me with his right hand. "Come here!" he ordered.

Uh-oh. What have I done? Coach had always been the disciplinarian type who was a stickler for details.

"Your helmet isn't on right," he said. With that, he made a fist with his right hand and punched down on the top of my helmet. The forceful slam pushed my batting helmet down around my head for a much snugger fit.

"Get your head in the game," he snapped. "This is no ordinary pitcher! You're not even ready to hit!"

I couldn't believe this was happening.

"I am too!" I yelled back—with respect. I wanted Coach Hoover to know that my head *was* in the game, even if my batting helmet wasn't on as tight as he thought it should be.

"Then show me!" he growled.

I stepped up to the plate, determined to demonstrate to Coach Hoover and my teammates that I could hit one of our best pitchers. I took several warm-up swings and concentrated on Steve Slaton's right arm as he went through his pre-pitch routine. When he delivered the first pitch—a fastball over the plate—I went after it. I swung and drove the ball to the left-centerfield wall, arriving at second base with a stand-up double.

I stood on second base and clapped my hands, fired up by my

line drive to left-center. Then I sneaked a glance at Coach Hoover. He, too, was clapping—and shaking his head in appreciation. He was probably thinking that he'd seen it all in baseball until this Springer kid came along.

Based on that double, I got a start in the next game against Orange Coast College, played on the road in Costa Mesa. We had clinched a spot in the playoffs, so the last couple of regular season games didn't mean a whole lot, which is why Coach had two Springers written down on his lineup card. My parents were thrilled beyond words to be in the grandstands watching us both play on the left side of the infield—Gary at short and me at third base.

I flew out in my first at-bat, and then in the bottom of the fifth, I hit a moon shot to right-center, easily clearing the fence. My home run trot—I hadn't had too many of those—was the most fun I'd ever had on a baseball field. I thoroughly enjoyed every single step. Since my blast came midway through the game, there wasn't a welcoming committee at home plate, but I exchanged plenty of high fives and received a bunch of pats on the butt in the Rustlers dugout.

The other Springer highlight that season happened to my brother. In recognition of his excellent play, Gary was named to the second team in the All-Southern Cal Conference, which earned him a trip to Anaheim Stadium—home of the California Angels (as the team was called back then) for a junior college All-Star game pitting players from Northern California and Southern California.

You can only imagine the excitement in the Springer household that Gary was going to play in a MAJOR LEAGUE STADIUM! The entire Springer family gathered in the field level seats to watch Gary play on the same dirt as Rod Carew, Don Baylor, and Bobby Grich of the Angels . . . plus all the American League stars who came into town: Reggie Jackson, George Brett, Fred Lynn, and Robin Yount. Watching

Gary play on the same major league field as those superstars boggled my mind.

Would I ever get the same experience—playing baseball in a 50,000-seat stadium? Sure, only several thousand attended the junior college All-Star game, but still, as I watched Gary take his position at shortstop, I wondered what it would be like to sneak a quick glance at the sea of seats and imagine being a major league baseball player.

I'm going to be there one day, I thought. I had no reason to entertain that thought, but I did that day. I knew I was a good baseball player. There was never a time when I thought, *You're just not good enough.* Others may have believed that, but I never did. I just needed to grow a little bit and get stronger. Now that I was 5 feet, 10 inches, I was an adequate height for an infielder. I had grown 11 inches since the start of my freshman year of high school.

I played a bit more and finished the season with eight at-bats and two hits, so even though I was still a .250 hitter, I was upbeat about my future. The good thing about junior college baseball was the big turnover in the team roster every year as sophomores either went on to a four-year school or hung 'em up. Of the twenty-four players on the Golden West roster, only seven freshmen would be returning for their second and last year of junior college baseball.

When the season was over, Gary was recruited by several big schools and accepted a full-ride scholarship to the University of Oklahoma, so he was on his way. That goes to show you how highly regarded junior college baseball in Southern California was viewed by college coaches around the country.

Gary received his A.A. degree after two years at Golden West and was accepted into the University of Oklahoma. Meanwhile, I was sinking deeper into academic quicksand. For the spring semester, I signed up for the following class load:

- Writing Center Practicum
- Violence in Films
- History of Rock 'n' Roll
- Strength Conditioning
- Baseball Team
- Comparative Governments
- Intro to Personal Communication

On the face of it, that was an aggressive class load, especially during baseball season. I'm afraid I was like a Vegas gambler, chasing losses with another big bet that I could perform in the classroom as well on the baseball field.

I didn't go bust and need bus fare to get home, but it wasn't pretty. I lasted in Writing Center Practicum about a month and pulled the ripcord, taking a W. Ditto for Comparative Governments—another withdrawal. When I failed to write papers for Violence in Film and Intro to Personal Communication, I received NCRs, meaning no credit because my work was unsatisfactory. Actually, my professors had taken pity on me; they could have given me D's or F's. The only non-P.E. class I passed was History of Rock 'n' Roll, in which I received a B.

My dad, who'd been on my case my whole life about getting good grades, reminded me for the umpteenth time that I needed to knuckle down and study—or get some tutoring help. Dad was like the proverbial canary in the coal mine, but I didn't want to listen.

With Gary's departure, a spot opened up at shortstop, his old position. This was my last chance to prove myself, and I wasn't going to let it slide by.

I wanted to play baseball.

GETTING STRONGER

I threw myself into the opportunity to become the starting shortstop. For summer school, I signed up for Sports Conditioning and Weight Training (and received much-needed A's for the one-unit classes) and returned to the canoes at Disneyland. Dressed in my Davy Crockett britches with a coonskin hat, I stroked a paddle eight hours a day. The Disneyland rowing and Golden West weight training helped me develop a muscular chest, broad shoulders, and six-pack abs. I was getting a lot stronger.

I remember a moment when everything crystallized for me. Uncle Gary and our cousins were over at the house one Sunday afternoon for a barbecue and a swim a couple of weeks after the baseball season ended. I, along with my brother Gary, who was named after my mom's brother, always looked up to our uncle. My uncle started working at Disneyland shortly after the amusement park opened in 1955 and had been steadily promoted through the years to a major supervisory position at Frontierland. He was a very good athlete, a standout baseball player at Huntington Beach High School. Gary and I always say we got our athleticism from Uncle Gary and Mom—and not from Dad, as I've described earlier.

We gathered around the pool that early summer afternoon, hanging out while Dad flipped hamburgers and hot dogs on the grill. As I jumped out of the pool, Uncle Gary said, "Yeah, you've really filled out. You used to be a shrimp. Now look at you!"

I grinned from ear to ear. Uncle Gary always had a way of making me feel like a million bucks.

"Must be all that canoeing you're making me do," I joked.

"I knew that would be a good job for you." Then Uncle Gary's face brightened. "I bet you're faster than Gary now."

"Wait a minute! I heard that!" said a voice from the diving board.

That was my brother interjecting himself into the conversation. "Sure, Steve may be taller than me now, but he's not faster," Gary declared.

There were some family dynamics going on in that statement. The vibe that my parents always exuded was that Gary was the best athlete in the family, the one with the best hand-eye coordination, the quicker hands, and the fastest feet. Gary was the sibling that my parents put on a pedestal all my life, although with good reason. He had been a star three-sport athlete at Marina High and an All-Star shortstop at Golden West—and I had warmed a bench. But as we were nearing the end of our teenage years, I had surpassed him in height and thus was a bit bigger.

Little brother was growing up.

"I bet Steve can race you for a $100," Uncle Gary said, setting a trap that my brother stepped into. After all, Uncle Gary didn't say that he would bet $100 that I could beat Gary but that I would race Gary for $100 if given the chance.

Forget the hundred bucks; Gary took that as a challenge. We changed out of our wet bathing suits, and everyone watched us step onto Mar Vista for the big match race: Who was faster—Gary or me?

We agreed that the footrace would be from streetlight to streetlight—a distance of around 60 yards in the middle of Mar Vista.

Our entire family and friends gathered at the finish line while Uncle Gary escorted us to the starting streetlight. I had never beaten Gary in a race in all my life. Though it had been years since we faced off, something told me I could take him.

Uncle Gary raised his arm. "Ready?"

I looked at my uncle and nodded.

"Get set . . . go!"

Gary and I left the starting line at the same time. I pumped my legs and arms like pistons. I heard my sisters and cousins yelling and screaming our names. The finishing light pole was coming up. I knew I had a step on Gary. I pushed myself to the limit—and beat him by a full stride.

Gary, as I expected, wasn't a good loser. "You cheater! You went early!"

I won fair and square. For the first time ever, I had conquered Gary the Great, and that felt really good.

SUMMER LEAGUE

I didn't have to try out for the Golden West summer league team since I was a returning player. At our first practice, Coach Hoover barked out names and told the players where to go.

"Springer—take shortstop," he said.

The only time I played shortstop was for the Disney softball team—and never in a real baseball game. But I wasn't going to tell Coach Hoover that. If playing shortstop is what it took to get me on the field, I wasn't going to say a word. Maybe Coach felt comfortable with having another Springer at the No. 6 position.

I jogged out to my new position to take infield. I may not have been the best infielder, but I did have a cannon for an arm. If there was a chopper between third base and shortstop, I could throw a dart to first base. I'd always had a good arm, but my throwing got a lot stronger when I added inches to my frame.

It sure felt good to be playing real baseball again—hardball instead of softball—and knowing that the starting position was mine.

Think about where I was during the summer of 1980. For the last two years, I had played in only a half-dozen baseball games: four or so at Marina High my senior year and a couple of games my freshman year at Golden West. At a time when I was in the prime of my development—eighteen and nineteen years old—I had been riding the pine and coaching first base instead of getting valuable on-the-field experience. I was watching baseball, not playing baseball.

Now I could turn that all around. My goal was to play as many games as I could at Golden West and see what happened. After all, if Gary got a full-ride scholarship to the University of Oklahoma, maybe I could play at a four-year school as well.

I wasn't finished dreaming of playing in the major leagues. Not by a long shot. The only thing I knew was that I didn't want my baseball career to end.

Now at Shortstop . . .

Wouldn't you know it—I grew another two inches between the end my freshman year at Golden West and the start of the 1981 season.

I marked my twentieth birthday in early February by measuring myself at the athletic training facility: I was officially 6 feet tall and weighed 170 pounds. I had to be the latest late bloomer in history. Remember, I was 4 feet, 11 inches when I started high school. A growth spurt of 13 inches between the time I was fourteen and twenty may not have been Jolly Green Giant stuff, but I had sprouted like a springtime weed.

We started playing non-league games in February. Every time I looked up, there were scouts or college coaches in the grandstands. Their presence didn't make me nervous at all. I *wanted* to play baseball so badly that any thoughts of performing poorly evaporated from my mind.

One afternoon, I was warming up my arm near the Rustler dugout when I overheard Coach Hoover talking to one of the college coaches.

"Who's your new shortstop?" the coach asked.

Coach Hoover raised the bill of his cap and shot a glance in my direction. "You mean him? That's Steve Springer."

The visiting scout thought he was fooling. "That's not Steve Springer. He's a lot smaller."

"You're right. It's not the same Steve Springer. He's four inches taller now, and you're going to like what you see."

I had always respected Coach Hoover. Now I loved him. Sure, I got my butt chewed more than a few times for being out of position or swinging at a bad pitch, but I still loved him.

I got out of the gate quickly my sophomore year. Throughout the season, I led the team in hits and hovered around the .333 mark. I showed power by hitting a lot of doubles and several home runs. Coach Hoover was suddenly receiving a lot more inquiries about his shortstop.

The University of California at Irvine baseball team was sniffing around. So was UCLA. Hearing that two public universities like UC Irvine and UCLA were interested in me—a benchwarmer the last two seasons—sounded unbelievable when Coach Hoover relayed the information.

"You think I got a shot, Coach?" I asked.

"Yeah, I do, but Irvine's a really big academic school. I think your transcripts might baffle them."

Okay, so I wasn't going to become a brain surgeon. I wasn't the greatest student, remember? In the fall, I decided to try another biology class along with a slew of classes in my favorite sports— baseball, golf, and badminton.

I couldn't hack Biology 101 and withdrew before I could get stuck with an F. So give me a W there. Of the "jock" classes I took, badminton was my favorite. I beat the No. 3 guy in the state like a drum—five times in a row. That made me the best badminton player at Golden West.

"Good job, Steve," said the teacher of the class, who also happened to be the coach of the Golden West badminton team. "We'd love to have you on the team this spring."

"Sorry," I said. "I've got baseball."

I also took classes that fall called Coaching Principles and First Aid/CPR: the former because maybe I'd want to get into coaching someday, and the latter because I might have the opportunity to save a life one day.

My other core class, called Intro to Personal Communication, was a bear. I caught a huge break when Andy Donegan, my old frosh-soph coach at Marina High and Gary's old football coach, was teaching the class. Actually, I signed up for the class precisely *because* Mr. Donegan was the teacher. I figured I needed this class to stay eligible. Unfortunately, my mid-term test was a disaster, so I was working on a D-minus in Intro to Personal Communications.

I decided to do some personal communications with Mr. Donegan and told him that I needed to get into C-minus territory so that I could be eligible for spring baseball. "You have to help me . . . please," I asked.

Thankfully, Mr. Donegan had a history with me. When I met him as a high school freshman, I wasn't much taller than 5 feet, so he had seen me metamorphose from a small-for-my-age caterpillar to a beautiful butterfly of baseball, trying to make my mark.

"I'll be waiting here for you when practice is over," said Mr. Donegan. Several times a week, Mr. Donegan tutored me on human interaction concepts. I may not have been the sharpest tool in the shed, but I eventually brought up my grade to a C-minus to stay eligible. I never felt prouder to get a crummy grade in my life.

With great trepidation, feeling like I was stepping into the Pacific Ocean and waiting for the dreaded "drop-off" into deeper waters, I gave it the old college try when signing up for my spring semester classes. My schedule looked like this:

- Intro to Nutrition
- Backpacking
- Weight Training
- Baseball Team
- Intro to Government

To show you how cavalier I was, I also signed up to play on the badminton team, figuring that I would show up for matches when they didn't interfere with baseball, but no such luck. I had to quit the team and withdraw from the class.

Intro to Nutrition proved to be out of my league. Chalk up another W there. Things didn't go much better with Intro to Government. After failing to produce any papers or class work, I strayed into NCR territory and received no credit. You have to understand that I didn't like to go to class. I know it sounds crazy to admit that, but I hated school. I just couldn't make myself go.

The only units I received credit toward a degree were for Weight Training and the Baseball team—four units. Thus, over the course of two years and four semesters at Golden West, I had accumulated just 41 units, or an average of 10 per semester. One needs to have 12 units a semester to be considered a full-time student.

Little did I know how big a price I would pay for my ineptitude in the classroom.

THE BRUINS COME CALLING

Sometime toward the end of the season, Mike Mayne, the head coach at Orange Coast College, received a phone call from Gary

Adams, the longtime baseball coach at UCLA.

Gary Adams got right down to business. "I need a shortstop, Mike. Who's the best in the area?"

"Steve Springer," replied Mike Mayne. "No doubt about it."

Even though I was academically incompetent, I was worthy of Honor Roll status as a baseball player. I put together a strong season and ended up playing in every game except for one. I batted a hefty .331 while leading the team in total hits with 44. Add three round-trip blasts to the total, and you can see why I was jazzed to play baseball at the expense of my studies.

Keep in mind that this was only my *third* season of organized baseball since middle school—and my *first* at the varsity level since I had played frosh-soph and JV ball in high school and no varsity baseball. Now that I was a starter at Golden West, I was squeezing every ounce of enjoyment out of playing college baseball as I could.

Just before my sophomore season wrapped up, I received a phone call at home following dinner.

"Hi, Steve. This is Gary Adams, the UCLA coach."

I nearly dropped the phone. Everyone in Southern California college baseball knew who Coach Adams was. We were equally versed in the storied Bruin baseball program. That spring the team had moved into Jackie Robinson Stadium, named after the first African-American baseball player to break the color barrier back in 1947 with the Brooklyn Dodgers. The Bruins were a big deal and always fielded a strong team in the Pac-10 conference, competing against marquee schools like USC, Stanford, Arizona State, and Cal Berkeley.

"Hi, Coach. Great to hear from you."

Coach Adams got to the point quickly. "We've been keeping an eye on you, young man, and we believe you'd be a good fit for the UCLA Bruin baseball program. How would like to join us in Westwood next fall? We're prepared to offer you a full athletic scholarship."

Did I hear right? Coach Adams wanted *me* to play for UCLA? On a full-ride? My dreams never went that far.

I didn't have to think twice about saying yes. "I'm coming!" I blurted. "What an honor."

Would someone wake me up? Tuition, books, and room and board? At UCLA? Did I just die and go to heaven?

"Excellent. We're counting on you, young man. There will be a few formalities. I'll have someone from the admissions department pull your transcript. All routine, I can assure you. And then we can look forward to having you play with us in the fall."

I thanked Coach Adams profusely and promised that he didn't make a mistake.

That night I dreamed about playing in a Bruins uniform with the iconic UCLA letters stitched across the top of the jersey. I can't remember if I hit a home run, but it didn't matter.

FLYING HIGH

I call it the greatest five days of my life.

When I told my parents that UCLA offered me a full-ride to play baseball, they didn't believe me at first. I didn't blame them. But after repeating my conversation with Coach Adams word-for-word three times, they finally allowed themselves to experience the same joy as I had.

The next day, Dad visited the Westminster Mall, where he found a sporting goods store selling UCLA ball caps and T-shirts. He must have bought the rest of their inventory because he came home with boxes and boxes of UCLA stuff. It looked like a lifetime supply. He joked about re-painting our house in dark azure blue and sun gold, the Bruin colors.

My brother, Gary, didn't believe me when we phoned him in Norman, Oklahoma, to relay the good news. I eventually convinced him that it was true—I was going to UCLA. I couldn't tell whether disbelief or jealousy colored his congratulations. He was having a great season too: he would be named to the second team of the Big 8 Conference in his first year with the Sooners despite a batting average of .244, a low for him. Gary was known for his fielding and his quick release.

When I wasn't on the field playing baseball for Golden West, I proudly wore my UCLA cap everywhere. Invariably, I had conversations like this with my friends:

"Hey, Spring. What's with the UCLA cap?"

"Didn't you hear? I'm playing for the Bruins next year."

"You're kidding! You're really going to play baseball at UCLA? How did that happen?"

"Beats me, but I can't wait to go."

I'm sure my friends were impressed. Why wouldn't they be? UCLA was a big deal in the Southland. My teammates were happy for me, just as I was happy for those who would be continuing their baseball careers at a four-year school.

Five days after Coach Adams offered me a UCLA scholarship, he called the house again after dinner.

I eagerly took the phone from my mom, who'd answered the call.

"What's up, Coach?" I began brightly. "I've been working hard. Can't wait to get there."

There was a long pause.

"Steve, that's going to be a problem. There's no way I can get you in here with your transcripts."

My world collapsed. "Oh," I managed.

"And I can get a lot of people in," he added.

Coach Adams wasn't rubbing salt in the wound. He was just

being matter of fact. "You didn't take the right classes. It's too late to do anything about it."

My heart sank to my stomach. I felt like such a loser. All I could think about was how embarrassing it would be telling my parents and my friends that I didn't get into UCLA. The first question my friends would ask would be "Why?"—and I would have to tell them the truth: I was a complete dummy in the classroom.

I'll admit that I was in a funk after that. My dad took the news just as hard as I did, but he didn't rub it in. He had admonished me for years that I needed to study more and get better grades—that my lack of effort in the classroom would come back to bite me one day—but I didn't want to listen to him. The day of reckoning had arrived, and it hurt.

Now that my college baseball career was over, I didn't know what I was going to do. I certainly wasn't going to continue going to college. Maybe I would make Disneyland a career. I could work my way up to Head Frontiersman or something like that. Maybe I could aspire to becoming a supervisor like my Uncle Gary.

I remember going to work at Disneyland the day after I got the devastating phone call from Coach Adams. It was such a drag paddling the canoes that day. Every time I dipped an oar in the water, I thought this was my destiny—circling Tom Sawyer Island like I was on an endless loop. *You better get used to it, bro, because you ain't going to college anymore.*

And then I got another phone call that changed my life.

8

Back to the Wall

A week after Coach Adams delivered the bad news, the phone rang after dinner. Shawn Gill was on the line.

Shawn was one my baseball buddies. He was a sophomore catcher on the Golden West team when I was a freshman and had gone on to play at the University of Utah, located in the capitol city of Salt Lake City. He had just finished playing his first season for the Utes.

"How'd you play?" I asked.

"Good," he said. "I really like it here in Utah, although it's a bit cold for me."

"How'd your season end up?"

"We didn't win the WAC championship, but we finished 15-9 in the conference and 23-20 overall, so not bad at all."

I knew that WAC stood for the Western Athletic Conference and included teams like the Air Force Academy, Brigham Young University, Colorado State, the University of Wyoming, the University of New Mexico, the University of Texas at El Paso (UTEP), San Diego State, and the University of Hawaii. They played some good baseball in the WAC Conference.

I prayed that Shawn wouldn't ask me how I was doing. Thankfully, he got right to the purpose of his phone call.

"Hey, we just lost our baseball coach, Mike Weathers. Long Beach State made him an offer he couldn't refuse. Lonnie Keeter is our new coach."

I wondered why Shawn was telling me all this "inside baseball" information. I mean, what did I care that two guys I never heard of were the new baseball coaches at Long Beach State and Utah? But then Shawn said something that made me sit up and take notice.

"Coach Keeter is playing catch-up on the recruiting front. He asked me if I knew anyone who could come play at Utah 'cause he has two more scholarships to give out. I brought up your name. Dude, you want to come to Utah?"

My face brightened. My baseball career was over, and suddenly I had been thrown a lifeline. "Yeah, but I probably can't get in," I said.

"Why's that?" Shawn asked.

"My transcripts are a mess. You should see them. Then again, maybe you shouldn't." Inwardly, I grimaced.

"Listen," Shawn said. "I know some of the football players here. They got into Utah, so if they can do it, I'm sure you can too."

Maybe all hope wasn't lost. "Okay, what do I do now?"

"I'll have Coach Keeter call you."

The next day, the new Utah coach phoned the house to introduce himself. I would later find out that Coach Keeter was young—just thirty-two years old—and the University of Utah was his first college coaching job. He seemed eager to please as well as easy to relate to.

We had a pleasant conversation, and he reiterated that he heard good things about me from Shawn and wanted to offer me a baseball scholarship. I immediately said, "Yes, I want to come," but I also described my debacle with UCLA. That didn't faze him. If anything, news that the Bruins wanted me enough to offer me a full-ride baseball scholarship left a good impression.

"I'm sure we can do something," he said. "You'll be hearing from us shortly."

When everything was said and done, the University of Utah admission department informed me that I was officially accepted, but I had to take a correspondence course that summer prior to enrollment in late August.

Hearing that caveat sounded ominous, but I was super motivated to pass this course in philosophy or psychology—I can't remember what it was. This time I knuckled down and put some effort into learning the class material. The Utah athletic department also arranged for a tutor named Eric, a little nerdy but a really good guy. With his help, I passed the correspondence class by the skin of my teeth. A big exhale. I was in.

Coach Keeter raided the Golden West roster for two more players who were close friends: Larry MacArthur, our second baseman, and Bob Grogan, our centerfielder. With Shawn Gill, that gave the Utes team a distinct Southern California flavor. What's even more amazing to me is that Lonnie Keeter gave me a scholarship without ever seeing me play. It was fully based on Shawn's recommendation.

Suddenly, paddling those canoes around Tom Sawyer Island that summer became a lot easier.

SAYING GOODBYE

*I*t was 5 a.m. and still dark when Larry MacArthur arrived at our Mar Vista home in his Ford truck. It was the middle of August. Ahead of us lay a twelve-hour journey of 700 miles to Salt Lake City, much of it across arid desert. Maybe we'd stop in Vegas and lose a few quarters in the slots.

I had just sold my orange-and-black Chevy Chevelle, a muscle car that wasn't suited for a snowy winter in the Wasatch Mountains. The transmission was shot and the gas-guzzler had been a lemon anyway, so I was glad to get rid of my well-used car just before leaving for school. Since I'd be living in a campus dorm a few miles east of downtown Salt Lake City, I didn't really need my own wheels in Utah's largest city of 1 million residents.

When Larry pulled up to our house in the predawn hours, Mom was still in her bathrobe as she watched me toss a couple of suitcases of clothes as well as a pair of cardboard boxes into the back of Larry's pick-up. As soon as I was loaded up, the tears started flowing down Mom's face. This was it—I was leaving home for the first time on a grand adventure. Then Mom lost it and started bawling, which made me glass up as well. I didn't want to cry in front of Larry.

We were roommates in the dorm room that we were assigned to. Larry and I were tight, and that helped us on the field because the bond between a shortstop and a second baseman always has to be close. It's easier to be successful at your position if you're working closely together.

We didn't have long to settle in before our first workout. I certainly wanted to impress Coach Keeter and his assistant coaches since first impressions are often lasting impressions. The first thing hitting coach Jerry Goyeneche did was take me into the batting cage to see what I could do. He stepped on the mound and threw me medium-pace fastballs. I hit each one on the screws.

Thwack.

Thwack.

Thwack.

Thwack.

Coach Keeter came by to have a look.

"He's everything as advertised, Lonnie," Coach Jerry said.

Next I warmed up my throwing arm and took my position at shortstop. Throwing had always been my best tool. My added height as well as all those paddle strokes in Rivers of America had built up my shoulders. I had as good of an arm as you can have.

After a few warm-up grounders and strikes to first base, I decided to show off a little. The next grounder, I threw the ball so hard that I snapped the leather webbing of Kenny Thompson's glove.

All in all, a good workout. I was gathering my gear and heading to the showers when I overheard Coach Goyeneche speaking with Coach Keeter.

"You better make sure this boy stays eligible," said Coach Jerry.

I guess word had made it to Salt Lake City that I wasn't an academic stalwart.

Word also got around quickly that you had better not go bowling or play pinball with me. I had the touch because my mom worked in a bowling alley from the time I was eight to fifteen years old, so I bowled and played pinball a lot after baseball practice and games were over. I could work a pinball machine for free games in no time at all.

Two of the football guys in our dorm, heavyset linemen Lindsey Gray and Darryl Haley, were always egging me on to win them free games on the pinball machine.

"Hey, Spring," said Lindsey, "I only have a quarter. Come win us some games."

"Stand back, boys," I'd say. "Don't touch the machine while I go to work." And then I'd win five free games for the guys and walk away a celebrity.

When the weather turned cold in October, we moved into a field house to practice. Well, it wasn't really a field house. More like a barn. As winter arrived, a few Kmart heaters struggled to keep the temperature inside the barn above freezing. It was brutally damp and cold in there. I wasn't used to seeing my breath with every exertion.

I had never lived in cold weather before. I'd only been in snow a couple of times when I went skiing at Mammoth Mountain in California's Eastern Sierra Mountains during high school. Mom made sure I had a good winter coat for Utah. I bought a pair of construction boots and wore those around campus to keep my feet warm.

On one frigid afternoon in November, I had a little setback. We were having an intersquad game inside the barn. Maybe I hadn't warmed up my arm the way I should have or maybe I needed to get a throw to first base with some heat on it. Whatever the reason, I felt a ripping pain in my upper right arm. As soon as the ball left my fingertips, I knew it wasn't good.

I grimaced as I held my throbbing arm. Coach Keeter ran onto the field to check on me. When he saw the great pain I was in, he escorted me to the dugout. "You're done," he announced. "You better get that looked at."

The training staff diagnosed a strained rotator cuff in my throwing shoulder and predicted that it would be several months before I could throw effectively again. I didn't want to hear that—not after I had come so far. Fortunately, I could still swing the bat.

Coach Keeter put my mind at ease. "We're going to make you our DH," he said, meaning I would be the designated hitter and not have to play a position in the field. My arm didn't hurt while hitting, just when I threw the ball. Thank God for the rule change in the DH back in 1973 or I would have been on the bench.

When I went home for the winter semester break, Dad—happy I was playing college baseball and happier that he wasn't paying one dime for my tuition, books, meals, and room-and-board—bought me a lime-green Honda Accord so that I could have some transportation. That was a really generous Christmas present.

After driving back to Utah following the holiday break, I met some cute girls. The one who caught my eye was Jerri. We got to know each other in volleyball class—yup, my class schedule was filled with assorted "rec" courses—but she broke my heart when she said she wouldn't go out with me because she had a boyfriend already.

While that was a let down, that was nothing compared to my class schedule . . . which was a ticking time bomb. I had skated by the skin of my teeth the first semester and barely stayed eligible. As baseball season got under way and we started traveling a lot, I generally skipped all my classes and rarely did any assignments. I still hated school. I just wasn't cut out to be a student and was lousy at studying.

I was a good hitter, though, which gave Coach Keeter a reason to keep my bat in the lineup as the Utes DH. I quickly established myself as the team's best hitter—for average and for power—raking base hit after base hit from Fort Collins to Colorado Springs to Laramie. In a four-game series against the University of Wyoming, I went 8-for-15 at the plate with a double, two triples, and a home run, accounting for 16 total bases.

While I was DH-ing, a talented freshman named Mike Dandos played shortstop and did a good job. When my arm eventually returned to full strength, Coach Keeter asked me if I could play in the outfield to keep Mike in the lineup. Like the trooper I am, I said yes, even though I was a terrible outfielder.

Coach stuck me in left field, figuring that's where I could do the least amount of damage.

BATTLE WITH BYU

*Y*ou know how colleges have "rivalry" games?

I'd grown up with the USC and UCLA rivalry. The *Los Angeles Times* always called the annual Trojans-versus-Bruins football game the "Crosstown Rivalry" or the "Battle of L.A."

In Utah, the University of Utah and Brigham Young University in nearby Provo were huge rivals in the Beehive State. Every fall the two football teams participated in the "Holy War" for bragging rights. Things weren't quite as heated on the baseball field, but I soon learned that the passion index shot up a few notches whenever the Utes and the Cougars squared off.

There was another dynamic in play. In this Mormon state, Brigham Young always got the best players, no matter what the sport. Every guy on my Utah baseball team, except for the four out-of-state players from Golden West, came from Mormon families and had been passed over by BYU. Understandably, my teammates had chips on their shoulders whenever we faced the Cougars. Each year, the rival teams played each other six times, but it had been a long time since Utah had beaten Brigham Young in baseball more than once in a season. For many years, the baseball version of the "Holy War" hadn't been much of a rivalry.

Utah was in the Northern Division of the WAC Conference with Brigham Young, Air Force, Wyoming, and Colorado State. As the 1982 season came to an end, we had a lot riding on a two-game series against BYU, which was 19-3 in the conference and 42-15 overall. We were struggling with a 16-28 overall record, but we had also begun the season 1-11, losing to the likes of Gonzaga, Lewis-Clark, and Southern Utah State.

We turned things around when conference play started and were in the race for a spot in the WAC baseball playoffs that pitted the top two teams from the Northern and Southern Divisions. If we could beat BYU at least once, we would finish no worse than 12-12 in conference play and tie the Air Force Academy for second place, but we would win the tiebreaker since we had won the season series against the Falcons.

Oh, did I mention that the WAC Championship would be hosted by the University of Hawaii in Honolulu, the best team in the Southern Division? I'd never been to Hawaii before, so the thought of playing baseball in the shadow of Waikiki Beach was very exciting.

But first we had to take one of the two games against BYU, the class of the WAC. We did just that in the first game, winning 2-1 in the bottom of the ninth when Mike Barnett hit a walk-off double with the bases loaded. We celebrated like we had won the College World Series in Omaha, Nebraska. Our players sprinted off the bench to home plate and dove into a mass of bodies like it was a dog pile. Not only had we defeated BYU for the second time in the season—a first in many years—but we were also going to Hawaii for the WAC playoffs.

There was still one more game to play the following day against the Cougars—in Provo, forty-five miles to the south. This collegiate baseball game would prove to be the most important one in my college career.

On the mound for the Cougars was their best pitcher, Pete Kendrick, a 5-foot, 8-inch left-hander from Honolulu. Earlier in the season I had gone 2-for-2 with two walks against Kendrick in our other victory against BYU, so I was confident that I could have another good game.

Kendrick was among *thirteen* players on the BYU team who would be drafted by Major League Baseball. Four of those players who would reach the major leagues:

- Rick Aguilera, who'd forge a 16-year career in the major leagues as a pitcher for the New York Mets, Minnesota Twins, Boston Red Sox, and Chicago Cubs.

- Wally Joyner, who'd also play for 16 years, most notably with the California Angels, where he was an American League All-Star.

- Cory Snyder, who'd played nine years, mainly with the Cleveland Indians, including a season when he hit 33 home runs.

- Scott Nielsen, a pitcher for the New York Yankees and Chicago White Sox for two seasons.

The Cougars' other pitching ace was Kevin Towers, who would be the San Diego Padres' No. 1 pick in the secondary phase of the 1982 Major League Baseball Draft. Although arm injuries stopped Towers from pitching in the big leagues, he went on to become a successful general manager with the Padres and Arizona Diamondbacks.

Such incredible talent drew a lot of scouts. On a cloudless Saturday in early May, more than fifty major league scouts were in the BYU grandstands to evaluate BYU's bumper crop of baseball talent. Truth be told, we didn't have any major league prospects, although I secretly hoped I would become one.

Pete Kendrick took a 11-2 record with him to the mound; he'd been practically unbeatable for his entire college career and had hurled two no-hitters during the 1981 season, when he won more games (16) than any BYU pitcher in history.

In my first at-bat, batting third, I took Kendrick downtown for a two-run homer to give us a short-lived 2-0 lead. For the rest of the game, I was a one-man offense for the Utes: I banged out a double, single, another single, and a double in my next four at-bats, but we only scored two more runs and came up on the short end of a 12-4 loss.

After the 5-for-5 day, I finished the season with a .387 batting average, best on the team, and had blasted six home runs, also a team high. In conference play, I really tore it up: I batted .440 and terrorized WAC pitching. I was stoked to hear that I was named to the All-WAC Conference team as the designated hitter.

Now, you may be wondering if this was an outlier season. Why had I jumped from batting .250 in my senior year of high school to .331 in junior college to .387 in a major Division I conference—in just three years?

The reasons are twofold. First, I was playing with a new body—one that was a solid 6 feet with 170 well-defined pounds. I could play baseball with a new strength I had never enjoyed before. Second, I always believed I had the ability to compete at the next level. Now I had a "man body" to match that desire.

This is when thoughts surfaced about playing pro baseball. Going into the 1982 season, I had no reason to think along those lines, but I also knew that players with numbers a lot worse than mine got drafted. The fact is that the Major League Baseball draft had forty-seven rounds, meaning close to 900 players got selected. I didn't think there were 900 junior and senior college baseball players or high school prospects better than me. (Freshman and sophomore college players are ineligible for the Major League draft.)

At some point during the 1982 season, I mentally placed all my eggs in the baseball basket. I didn't think I could hack another year in school—or stay eligible.

A DOG DAY

*F*ollowing my big day in Provo, we had a week before we hopped on a flight to Honolulu for the WAC Championships. The day before our departure, I was packing up in my dorm room when my new roommate Todd Fritchman slapped his forehead. Todd was a pitcher on our team and was known as a bit of an airhead.

"Dog, I can't believe I forgot to tell you!"

My nickname, for some reason, was "Spring Dog" on the Utah team, which often got shortened to "Dog."

"Tell me what?" I asked.

"Some scout from the Cincinnati Reds called. He invited you to a workout."

This was exciting news. A workout meant he wanted to take a closer look at my baseball skills so that he could evaluate whether I was worthy of being drafted. "Do you know when the workout is?" I inquired.

"It was yesterday."

My heart sank. The workout was history—long gone.

"Sorry, man," he said. "I forgot."

I was too bummed to say anything. Of course, Todd hadn't asked for the scout's name or his telephone number.

When the Reds didn't call back, all I could think about for the next couple of days was this: *There goes my only shot to get drafted by a major league team.*

Draft Time

The trip to Hawaii was great. I loved the "aloha" spirit and laid-back vibe. I told myself that I could get used to playing baseball in tropical surroundings real quick.

Of the four teams in the WAC Championship, we had the worst record by far—and were the least experienced. The University of Hawaii and San Diego State, the top two finishers in the Southern Division, both competed in 70 ballgames. We had played only 46 games before the season-ending WAC playoffs.

In Honolulu, we quietly lost both games in the double-elimination tournament and were done. Our consolation prize was hitting Waikiki Beach for a day of R&R before we flew home. While the host team, Hawaii, took the WAC Championship, my older teammates and I discovered "umbrella" drinks at the poolside lounge. (I had turned twenty-one back in February.)

After returning to Salt Lake City, I packed up my belongings and drove home for the summer, where the canoes in Frontierland were waiting for me—as well as an uncertain future. Would I be drafted? I had no idea. If no major league club selected me, I was worried that I wouldn't be academically eligible for my senior year. Was the Disneyland softball team my last stop on a baseball diamond?

The Major League Amateur Draft started on June 5, 1982, a Saturday. I wondered if I was on any team's draft board, but I doubted it. No scouts had contacted me. No teams had asked me for a private workout after the Cincinnati Reds mess-up. No agents had called, asking if they could represent me.

I held out hope that a team would take a flier on me. I had good numbers. Okay, maybe I didn't bat .445 like Wally Joyner did while playing first base at Brigham Young, but .387 was nothing to sneeze at either. I was All-WAC as the designated hitter, which had to count for something.

Truth be told, I wasn't the only Springer hoping to get drafted. Gary had just finished his senior season at the University of Oklahoma and put up draft-worthy numbers: a .301 batting average with 14 doubles, two home runs, and 35 RBIs. He'd also been named to the second team in the All-Big 8 Conference.

So there was a fleeting hope in our household that one or both of us would be drafted. That weekend, Gary and I hung around the house, hoping to hear the phone ring.

In those pre-Internet days, that's all you could do—sit around and wait. ESPN wouldn't broadcast the Major League Draft until 2007. Then a baseball friend of Gary's called the house and spoke to my brother. He said that he had heard through the grapevine that Gary had been drafted. By which team or in what round he didn't know.

There were whoops in the house. I wasn't jealous at all that Gary got drafted. In fact, I thought this was good news for *me*. If Gary got picked, then I had a good chance of getting selected because of my higher batting average.

We needed more information. Dad suggested calling Dick Cole, a major league scout that he had chatted with through the years. Dick was local, and we had his phone number.

I watched with anticipation as Gary picked up the phone. His hands were practically trembling as he dialed the number. When he finished, I got on the other phone in the house to listen in.

"Hello, Mr. Cole? This is Gary Springer. Yes, I'm doing fine. We heard from a friend that I got drafted. Do you know anything?"

"Yeah, hold on," the scout said. "I got the list right here." There was a delay as he scanned the names on the list.

"Here it is," said the scout. "Springer from Utah. New York Mets. Twentieth round."

Springer from Utah?

That meant *I* got drafted, not my brother, who played at Oklahoma. I couldn't believe what I just heard. Naturally, I was ecstatic, but I was careful not to go overboard since Gary hadn't been drafted yet. In fact, he would not be selected in any of the forty-seven rounds, which put a damper on the celebration at Mar Vista.

Eventually, I received a phone call from someone with the Mets organization confirming that I *had* been drafted by the New York Mets and that I could expect to receive a contract offer in the next day or two.

So how did I get picked?

When we played Brigham Young in the last WAC conference game of the season in Provo, one of the fifty scouts in the grandstand was Roy Partee, a longtime New York Mets scout. He'd played five years in the major leagues as well as in the 1946 World Series with the Boston Red Sox. He wasn't in Salt Lake City that day to scout me, of course. He was tracking blue chippers like Wally Joyner and Rick Aguilera.

Then he watched an unknown go 5-for-5 against a talented

pitcher like Pete Kendrick, which made him sit up and take notice.

A few days after the draft, a trio of Mets scouts—Harry Minor, Bobby Minor, and Dean Jongewaard—dropped by the house. Dad, Mom, Gary, and I were waiting for them.

We gathered around the coffee table in the living room and made small talk.

"Looks like it could be Angels' year," one said.

"Yup, could be," Dad allowed.

Our hometown Angels, bolstered by the free-agent acquisition of Reggie Jackson, were in first place in the American League West.

"Yeah, as long as Bobby Grich can keep up his hitting," chimed in another scout.

My father lost his patience. "You know, you're signing the wrong guy," he said.

Time stopped as all heads swiveled toward my dad.

"What do you mean?" asked Harry Minor.

"Gary's the one you should be signing," my father said. "He's got more talent than anyone in this family. Take him. You'll be glad you did."

There were several awkward glances and a cough or two until Harry Minor spoke again. "I appreciate that you feel this way, Mr. Springer, but we're here to sign Steve. Hopefully Gary will get his chance someday."

I breathed a heavy sigh of relief. For a moment there, I thought the Met scouts were going to stand up and leave.

Bobby Minor met my gaze. "Steve, we realize that you have one more year of eligibility at the University of Utah, so we're prepared to offer you a $4,000 signing bonus if you will forgo your senior year and join the Mets organization as a professional baseball player."

What sweet words to my ears . . . *professional baseball player.*

After hearing Bobby Minor state it like that, I was going to sign no matter what they offered. Besides, I knew I wasn't cut out for college and might not be academically eligible anyway. This was my greatest break ever. But maybe I could ask for a little more money.

"Can I get $5,000?" I asked. It was worth a try.

"No," Bobby Minor said without any hesitation.

I laughed, which eased the tension in the room. "So where do I sign?" I asked.

Dean Jongewaard reached into his briefcase. "Here's our standard minor league contract," he said as he handed a sheaf of papers over to me. "We have several incentive clauses. If you spend ninety days in Double-A, you'll get a $1,000 bonus. Ninety days in Triple-A, and you'll get $1,500. And if you're in the major leagues for ninety consecutive days, you'll get another $5,000. We also give you a year of school."

A year of school? The last thing I wanted to do was go back to the classroom.

"What's that?" I asked.

"It's like a $10,000 insurance policy," said Dean Jongewaard. "If you get released, you have up to two years to go back to school, and we'll pay the first $10,000 of your education costs."

"I don't think I'll be needing that." I flashed a quick smile to my dad.

"That's for sure," Gary said, getting in a big-brother jibe.

I grinned, but I wasn't going to mess around any longer.

"Sign right here, young man," said Dean Jongewaard.

With a stroke of the pen, my dream to play in the major leagues was alive and real.

ROOKIE BALL

The next day, I boarded a flight at LAX for a series of flights to the East Coast. My destination: Little Falls, New York, where I would be joining the Mets affiliate in the New York-Penn League, a Class A Short Season league that started in June after the amateur draft. I was accompanied by Joe Redfield, a 10th round pick of the Mets from the University of California at Santa Barbara. Joe would be the very first guy I met in pro baseball, and we're still great friends today.

We landed in nearby Utica, where the Mets affiliate was playing that night against the Utica Blue Sox, an independent team. I didn't expect to play, of course, but then my new manager, Sam Perlozzo, found me on the bench at the top of the ninth inning. "Springer, you're pinch-hitting."

I took some warm-up swings in the on-deck circle and looked at my bat. It was a wooden Louisville Slugger CT71, 34 inches long and weighing 32 ounces. I hadn't hit a baseball with a wood bat since my over-the-line days on Penfield Circle. From Little League all the way through to Utah, I had swung an aluminum bat.

Aluminum bats, lighter and stronger than wood, were banned in professional baseball because the ball springs off the barrel with a higher velocity—kind of a trampoline effect. The result: more home runs, higher batting averages, and the possibility of severely hurting pitchers and infielders.

I had talked with some of my new teammates about transitioning from aluminum to wood, and a couple of them warned me about swinging the bat differently when making the switch. I vowed to keep the same swing through the hitting zone. During batting practice that night, I think I figured everything out. A bat is a bat, right?

I took my stance, and I was sitting on a fastball—and I got it.

I swung from my heels and hit a medium-deep high fly ball to left field that hung in the night air for a long time—seven seconds. As the left fielder settled under the high fly ball, I kicked the dirt after rounding first base. I had just got under the pitch—one grain of the bat from hitting a home run in my first professional at-bat.

The next day, we had a team picnic in Little Falls, twenty-five miles east of Utica. Minor league players often live with "host families," and that was the case with me. A woman named Mary opened up her home, but she established some ground rules right off the bat: I had to be in at certain times and no shoes in the house. Since she lived a half-mile from the stadium, I didn't need a car.

Joe Redfield stayed with the Lewis family, and they had three little boys who looked up to the "baseball star" living with them that summer. The Lewis family sort of adopted me, and I ate lunch every day at their house before going to the ballpark.

At the team picnic, I met Bobby Valentine, who'd retired a few years earlier after a ten-year career in the big leagues. He would eventually become a successful manager with the Mets in the mid-1990s, but that summer, he was a roving instructor.

Bobby sat down on a park bench next to me and dove into a hamburger fresh off the grill. "You're going to play center field and lead off tomorrow," he said between bites. "I can tell just from the way you swung the bat last night that you're a ballplayer. In fact, you're my pick to click," he said.

My chest swelled with pride. That was cool to hear. But did the Mets organization know that I wasn't an outfielder? Roy Partee had scouted me that one game when I played left field against BYU, so he had no clue I was in the outfield to keep Mike Dandos in the lineup at shortstop and that I was really an infielder. Since Bobby had been so complimentary of my batting skills, I decided to level with him.

"Just so you know, I've never played center field in my life," I said. Bobby wasn't fazed at all. "Just fake it then," he said.

In the bottom of the first inning, I led off with a walk. Eight batters later, we were still batting. Now the bases were full.

I saw a fastball I liked and turned on it. This time I wasn't a grain off. The baseball jumped off my bat and easily cleared the center field fence.

Grand slam home run!

As I rounded the bases, I could barely keep a straight face. I was so happy after all the years of people and coaches telling me that I was too small to play baseball and would never make it. And now my first professional hit was a grand slam home run—what a feeling! With such an auspicious start, I knew I was going straight to the big leagues. The stars were aligned, right?

Bobby Valentine was sitting in the bullpen and had the home run ball brought to him. That night, when the game was over, I discovered the ball in my locker. I called home collect to share the excitement—and learned some even better news: Gary had been picked up by the Detroit Tigers as a free agent.

Roger Jongewaard, Dean's brother, was a long-time scout with the Tigers. He must have heard the "You're signing the wrong guy" story and figured Gary came from a family with some chutzpah. Roger offered Gary $500 to sign, but I think my brother would have paid the Tigers organization five hundred bucks for a chance to play professional baseball. Now he had a shot at reaching the big leagues. First stop: the Bristol Tigers, the rookie-level Single-A team in Bristol, Virginia.

A great day for the Springers. I wish I could have seen the joy in the faces of my parents. They had to be thrilled beyond words that both their sons were playing professional baseball.

A LOT OF BASEBALL

*I*ended up playing the entire season in left field, where I wasn't very good. I did okay in the batting department: I hit .246 but showed good power by belting 11 home runs in 67 games with 38 RBIs.

But I got so tired. I had never played so much baseball in such a short amount of time. Think about it: up until I turned pro, I had played, at the most, fifty or sixty baseball games in the last three years. Now I had been in the lineup for 67 games in *ten weeks!* There was another thing I had never thought about: it's hard to keep your head screwed on straight day after day. I suddenly had a greater appreciation for what professional baseball players—at any level—have to do to prepare their bodies physically and mentally for the rigors of playing this great game every day.

I remember the last day of the season. If I could get two or three hits, I could hit .250 and reach a psychological milestone. Midway through the game, I hit a high chopper to shortstop. I thought I could beat the throw. I was moving down the line really good and was steps from the bag when—

—I pulled every muscle in my lower back.

I hit the dirt in a heap and never made it to first base. A pair of trainers helped me off the field. I took baby steps because of the pain.

I spent the next day on Mary's couch. Whenever the phone rang, I couldn't get off the couch to answer. I was hurting.

It was a couple of days before I boarded a flight for Salt Lake City, where Mike Barnett and Shawn Gill, teammates of mine on the University of Utah team, picked me up at the airport. I had a great time hanging out with them and other college friends. Shawn, my old roommate, had been picked up by the Oakland A's and just finished his first season of rookie ball.

Shawn and I returned to Huntington Beach, where Gary was waiting for us. My brother was back from Bristol, where he nosed me out with a .251 batting average but hit just one home run in 58 games. None of us were asked by our parent organizations to be part of the Florida Instructional League, where young major league prospects hone their skills from the end of September through October.

Notice I said the word *prospects*. Shawn, Gary, and I weren't asked because we weren't considered to be strong candidates to reach the major leagues.

The three of us talked about it and decided there was only one thing we could do: get to the gym and start working on getting bigger and stronger.

We would have to make our own opportunities. Now that baseball was my job—a profession—I needed to be professional.

10

A Throw in the Dirt

I made $600 a month playing in Little Falls and collected three paychecks during the short season, so I earned $1,800 that summer. I think I came home with a $1,000, but I was thrilled. Even though I was paid peanuts, I felt like the richest guy in the world because I never had a thousand bucks to my name before. Since free agency in baseball was only a few years old in the early 1980s, the escalating salaries didn't apply to Gary and me because we were minor leaguers.

That said, it was a good thing Gary and I could save a few bucks by moving back into our old bedrooms on Mar Vista and eating Mom's one-dish meals. It would be a full house as Susan and Robin were still living at home while attending Long Beach State and Golden West College, respectively, and then there was our little sister, the fifth child.

My parents had a "surprise baby" when I was in my sophomore year of high school. We got teased a bit by our friends because my mom and dad had another child at their age, but that didn't matter to us. We loved our sister Cori the minute she arrived. Mom took Cori to every game that Gary and I played in as well as all my sisters' games and events when she was a toddler. Let's just say she was a very popular little kid! When Gary and I returned from our first season in pro baseball, Cori was an energetic first-grader who kept everyone young.

I needed to earn some money, so I worked for a good friend, Jan Bagnall, who owned Galahad Decking. I can't say I was really into building decks on balconies. Sometimes I'd show up at the job site at 10 a.m. and my first question would be, "When are we eating lunch?" Gary got a job cleaning carpets for Chem-Dry with his good buddy Mark Dapello, the younger brother of our old babysitter, Mike Dapello.

Several afternoons a week Gary and I would knock off work early and work out at the Golden West baseball field with our ex-teammate Shawn Gill. We'd throw, take batting practice off each other, and hit each other ground balls to hone our fielding skills. Then we'd go to the weight room and lift. Each of us had to get bigger and stronger.

And then we'd meet friends at one of the Huntington Beach bars near the coast, where the pitchers of beer kept coming. We kept "baseball hours," meaning that we were rarely in bed before midnight. Staying up late—and chasing girls—was part of the baseball lifestyle, and since we were ballplayers, that's what we did. At least that's what we told ourselves at the time. No wonder I had trouble arriving at work before 10 a.m.

When February came around, I reported for spring training at St. Petersburg, Florida, hoping to be promoted to the Mets Single-A team, the Columbia Mets in Columbia, South Carolina. The Columbia team belonged in the South Atlantic League, which everyone called the "Sally" league. More than a dozen Single-A teams stretching up and down the Atlantic Seaboard from Salisbury, Maryland, to Rome,

Georgia, comprised the Sally League.

I barely made the Columbia Mets as the fifth outfielder, which meant I was back on the bench. But at least I was out of rookie ball. To celebrate, a new baseball buddy, Mark Carreon, and I hit a bar in Tampa advertising "nickel beer night." Mark, an outfielder, was also 6 feet tall and 170 pounds.

Picture the scene that evening: a typical bar, noisy and packed, filled with testosterone-fueled males and beautiful females drinking their five-cent draft beers one after another. Mark started chatting up a pretty young woman. Suddenly, her boyfriend appeared and said he didn't appreciate that sort of thing.

Mark told him to pound sand, and that's when the brawl started. Tables tipped over as the two wrestled and tumbled to the floor. Punches were thrown, and it became apparent that my buddy was getting his butt kicked.

I dove into the melee to break things up. I hit the floor and was on my knees when I suddenly saw stars. One of the boyfriend's buddies kicked me in the head with his cowboy boot, opening a big gash in my eye.

I nearly passed out as blood streamed down the side of my face. Order was restored, but I needed medical attention. A girl I met that night took me to the local hospital, where an ER physician knitted ten stitches above my eye to close the wound.

The next day, I saw the Mets minor league trainer. He took one look at me and didn't have to ask if I had been in a fight the night before. He reported the stitches to Steve Schryver, the Mets farm director, and that's when I knew I was in trouble. Schryver was a no-nonsense, tough, and demanding baseball executive.

When I stepped into his office, he laid into me. "Are you kidding? Getting into a fight? You barely made it to A ball! I'm thinking about sending your butt to Little Falls until you're mature enough to stay out of fights."

I stood there and accepted the verbal abuse. I didn't want to throw Mark under the bus, so I just wore it.

"I promise it won't happen again, Mr. Schryver," I said.

The farm director gave me one more chance.

When I arrived in Columbia, there was a "Meet the Mets" promotion downtown for the local townspeople. I tugged my hat as low as I could to shield my black eye, but I'm sure my "shiner" didn't go unnoticed.

I didn't play the first month of the season—not because I got kicked in the head but because I was the fifth outfielder on the bench. Since I wasn't playing, I approached our manager, John Tamargo, and volunteered to coach first base.

"Coach, I have a lot of experience at that position," I said in a lighthearted way. "I've been coaching first all my life. I'm almost a pro at it."

Tamargo shook his head. I bet he never heard that request from a player before. "Go ahead. Be my guest," he said.

I eventually got to play a little bit in left field, but let's just say I didn't distinguish myself in the outfield.

On May 1, our second baseman got traded. I saw an opening and approached Tamargo in his office before a home game. We played at Capital City Park, built in 1927 and a real bandbox.

"Coach, let me play second," I began. "I've been an infielder my whole life. I'm telling you, I'm an infielder. That's the position I played in high school and junior college."

Tamargo looked up from the lineup card he was filling out. "Thank God because you suck in the outfield," he said.

I couldn't agree more. "I know! It's a long story, but I should have been drafted as an infielder. Let me show you what I can do," I said.

A few days later, I got a shot at second base—my first time in the infield in pro baseball. Everything was going pretty good until the eighth inning . . . when a double-play ground ball went right between my legs and we lost the game.

Tamargo sat me on the bench after that miscue, but I continued taking ground balls before games, which gave me a feel for the infield in Columbia.

A week later, I got a second start at second base. Once again, everything was going pretty good . . . until the eighth inning. That's when another double-play ball bounced through my legs into right field.

But I got four hits that day—and the flubbed double play didn't impact the final score.

As I learned in baseball, if you can hit, they'll find a place for you. I stayed in the lineup, continued hitting well, and ended up playing every single day for the rest of the season. I even led the Sally League in hits with 165—after not playing the first month of the season! After raking 50 hits in August, I finished the season second in batting average at .338. Vince Coleman, who'd later become a big league star, won the batting crown with a .350 average.

We qualified for the Sally League playoffs against the Gastonia Expos in Gastonia, North Carolina. Best of five games. After carrying the team for the last month, I felt like I was really contributing to our success. Losing our first two games on the road put our backs to the wall. We had to sweep a three-game series on our home field to claim the Sally League championship.

In Game 3, I had the game-winning hit to keep our season alive. In Game 4, the same thing—a game-winning hit. Now we were in the decider, Game 5, and up by a run in the top of the ninth. We had two outs, but there were runners on second and third. Our fans were on their feet, cheering us on to shut down a last-gasp rally.

Ground ball up the middle. This was my chance. I cut the ball off right before the second base bag, but I got an in-between hop. I had to get the ball out of my glove in a hurry to beat the runner. I didn't get as good a grip as I wanted, so I had to three-finger the throw to Dave Magadan, our first baseman, to end the game.

From the corner of my eye, I saw our guys coming out of the first base dugout, raising their hands. This looked like the game-winning out.

My throw ran out of steam and bounced just in front of Dave's outstretched mitt. I held my breath to see if he could pick the short-hop, but the ball bounced off the end of his glove. The tying run scored while Dave scrambled after the loose ball.

In the midst of confusion, the trailing Expos runner kept running past third base. He was going for home!

Everyone in the infield yelled for Dave to make the throw to the plate. Magadan, destined to reach the majors in three years and stay there until he was thirty-eight years old, grabbed the ball and fired a strike to home. The runner crashed into our catcher, Barry Lyons, which sent both bodies sprawling. But Barry hung on to the ball! The home plate ump, satisfied Barry still had the ball in his grasp, raised his right arm.

"You're out!" he screamed.

The collision at the plate prompted a great tradition—an old-fashioned baseball brawl. I ran toward home plate to back up my teammates and pushed a few Expo players around, but the umps quickly restored order.

We didn't score in the bottom of the ninth, so we had to go to extra innings. A Gastonia player hit a solo home run in the top of the 10th, so we had to get at least one run to stay alive. I started our rally with a base hit and took second on a bunt. Our next batter hit a little roller to the second baseman, which gave me time to reach third base.

Two outs. Me on third. Lou Horton, our centerfielder, was our last hope.

Strike one looking.

Strike two looking.

Strike three looking.

Lou never got the bat off his shoulder, and we lost the Sally League championship. And now I had to walk through their dog pile on my way to the dugout.

As I passed the celebration, I ached inside. This loss really hurt. We had come so close to winning the league championship. Even though I could have ended the game with a good throw to first, I didn't. It was a "tough chance," as they say in baseball, and sometimes baseball really is a game of inches.

The next day, I packed up for the flight home. As tough as the loss was, I felt some satisfaction since I had a great season in Single-A. As I looked ahead, I had only one thought in mind: I wanted a shot at Double-A.

I felt I could play at the higher level.

INSTRUCTION TIME

I had only been home for a few weeks when I left for the Florida Instructional League, which was by invitation only. It was too bad Gary didn't get to go. He spent the 1983 season playing for the San Jose Bees in Northern California. The Bees were a "co-op" Single-A team, meaning that several major league teams contributed players to the roster—including five from Japan—because there was no room for them on one of their minor league teams. Gary batted .254 in 128 games, which is probably why he wasn't invited to Instructional ball.

In Florida, the Mets farm director Steve Schryver met with me before the start of the six-week season. "We like how you throw the ball," he began, "so we're thinking that it's kind of a waste to play you at second base. We'd like you to play shortstop and see how that goes. Have you ever played that position?"

"Yeah, in my second year at Golden West," I said, leaving out the information that I led the league in errors my sophomore year. "Then I injured my arm at Utah and played a lot of DH."

"Good. I'm glad you're willing to give short a try."

So it was off to shortstop, knowing that I was not your prototypical player at that position. Shortstops are usually team leaders or the best player on the team. Growing up in the shadow of my older brother, I wasn't the team leader type like Gary or generally considered the best player on the teams I played on in the past. I had the strong arm—all those summers rowing canoes at Disneyland had paid off—but my fielding skills were average. When the ground ball was above my waist, I was fine, but if the ground ball was down at my feet, I got a little iffy.

Shortstops are naturals at the position, and I wasn't a natural shortstop like Gary. I didn't have the feet to play short, meaning my feet weren't quick enough to move into position to field the ball. I wasn't that great at reading hops.

But lastly, and this is most important, nearly all major league shortstops have played the position their entire lives, starting when they were eight years old. They had a fourteen-year jump on me since I was twenty-two. Plus, I hadn't played that much baseball anyway, as I've described. Even though I knew I would be competing against shortstops who'd played hundreds and hundreds of games at the position while I had maybe fifty games max under my belt, that wasn't going to stop me from trying. I was a "can do" person.

That said, I did okay playing shortstop in the Instructional League. If the shortstop position was going to be my ticket to the major leagues, then I was willing to work as hard as I could on my fielding, knowing that I had the arm.

But first, I had to climb up another rung on the ladder.

I set my sights on Double-A.

Dream On

When I went to spring training before the 1984 season, I walked with a bit more confidence into the Mets training facility.

I was a prospect, and there are no sweeter words for a young ballplayer trying to scratch and claw his way to the major leagues. I was in the mix because I had a great season at Single-A and more than held my own in Instructional League. After diligently lifting weights during the off-season with Gary and Shawn, I believed I was ready for a promotion to Double-A ball. I decided to press my case with farm director Steve Schryver the next time I saw him hanging around the batting cage.

With bat in hand, I approached him on a bright afternoon in St. Pete.

Schryver took his eyes off the field when he saw me. "Oh, hey, Spring. How ya doing? How was your off-season? Everything good?"

"Really good," I responded, but there was something else I wanted to discuss. "Hey, I was wondering if I could talk to you about my future. I don't mean to be an idiot, but I just led the Sally League in hits. I don't need another year of A ball."

Schryver took a closer look at me. Then he chuckled and walked away, lost in his thoughts. He didn't say a word to me.

Wow, that went great.

I didn't know if I had said something stupid—it wouldn't have been the first time—but on this occasion, my lobbying effort worked: the following day, I got word from Schryver that I had been assigned to the Jackson Mets, the club's Double-A affiliate in Jackson, Mississippi, home of the state capitol and Mississippi's largest city with 200,000 residents.

Before spring training camp broke, another incident happened, but this one shook me down to my cleats. One morning, while I was putting on my uniform, I felt something coming on in my head. Then my left eye closed up to the point where I could only see a slit of the world. I turned to my right to look at the guy dressing next to me. All I could see was his neck. The rest of his body was cut off.

Only my left eye was affected. My right eye was 100 percent okay. I was about to freak out when my vision returned to normal in my left eye. I shrugged my shoulders and continued with my day, but the incident scared the heck out of me.

A week later, I had the same experience: I felt a buzzing in my head and then I could only see a slit through my left eye. I was fine after a few minutes. Was I having these weird vision episodes because I got kicked near the eye on nickel beer night in Tampa? I wondered if that was the case.

A few days after that, during an intersquad game in St. Pete, I was standing in the batter's box when my head started feeling different again. Sure enough, I could only see through a slit in my left eye.

I could no longer hide my condition from the Mets. I called for time and stepped out of the batter's box and bent over, holding my head. A trainer ran out of the dugout. "I can barely see out of my left eye," I complained.

"Stand up straight and let me have a look at you," he said.

I squinted in the afternoon sun and felt woozy. "I have to sit down," I said.

The trainer wrapped an arm around my waist and escorted me off the field. This was serious. Someone would have to pinch-hit for me.

Inside the locker room, the trainer took a closer look, but he was mystified about what was wrong with me. Then the sight in my left eye returned in full, and I was fine again—like nothing had happened. The trainer wasn't satisfied by the fast turnaround.

"We're going to get you checked," he said.

"Sounds good to me," I said. I put on a brave face, but inwardly, I was scared. I even wondered if my days of playing baseball were over. Had I come this far—only to be sidelined by an acute vision problem?

It didn't seem possible.

The next day, the trainer found me in the locker room while I was suiting up. "I did some asking around, and we're going to send you to a specialist in New York," he said.

Now I knew this was serious. The Mets wouldn't put me on a flight from Florida to the team headquarters in New York unless they thought something was up.

I was taken to a Manhattan hospital, where various tests were run, including a spinal tap—a procedure that nearly did me in. Suddenly, I felt like I was walking around with an axe in my head. The pain was tremendous, like nothing I had ever experienced before. I couldn't move—and I didn't get better. The Mets didn't know what to do with me.

I ended up staying in the hospital for *ten days* while more tests were run. Specialists shined lights into my eyes and pressed and probed different pressure points in my head. Scans were done.

Finally, I heard a diagnosis: I had something known as a "painless migraine"—a type of headache that impacted my eyesight. They were also known as visual migraines, ocular migraines, or silent migraines. The symptoms—known as "auras"—were generally distorted vision in one or both eyes, vertigo or dizziness, and difficulty in speaking.

I was given a prescriptive medication, which seemed to help. I flew back to St. Pete just before the end of spring training. The following day, I felt another episode coming on, so I bent over like I was doing a "touch your toes" exercise. Putting my head below my waist prompted a rush of blood to the brain. My symptoms dissipated.

But if I stood up, I felt horrible. If I bent over, I felt better.

I figured out that I had to bend over for a good minute or two to keep the symptoms from returning. With that discovery, I now had a way of "treating" my painless migraines. Feeling like I turned a corner, I was ready to return to baseball. I drove to Jackson, where I moved into an apartment with pitcher Rick Aguilera and Billy Beane—yes, the Billy Beane who was played by actor Brad Pitt in the 2011 movie, *Moneyball.*

I missed the first two weeks of the season while I took it easy. When I returned to the starting lineup, I took my place at shortstop, but I felt like I needed a little more time to get my baseball skills back.

Sam Perlozzo, my manager in Little Falls, had been promoted to the Jackson Mets team. He had seen me butcher fly balls in the outfield, so I'm sure he was anxious about how I would perform at my new position. If I fielded a ground ball cleanly, I might throw it away, but I might not field the grounder in the first place. Once again, I depended on my bat to keep me in the lineup.

We had an excellent shortstop playing second base, Al Pedrique, a Venezuelan who'd been anchoring the left side of the infield since the second grade. He was a much better fielder than me, but I was the better hitter. I knew we would be a stronger team with Al at short and me at second base, so a month into the season, I approached Sam and suggested doing a switcheroo.

"Okay, we'll give it a try," he said. Moving me to second did make us a better team, but the 1984 Jackson Mets were loaded already. Nineteen of the thirty-one players who were on the roster would make it to the major leagues, including Lenny Dykstra, who was two years younger than me. Lenny had played at Garden Grove High School in nearby Garden Grove, so there was a Southern California kinship between us.

Looking back, though, my "team first" attitude may have hurt my chances of getting to the major leagues. I should have stayed at shortstop, learned from my mistakes, and learned how to play another vital position. But I wanted to win so badly, which is why I suggested to Sam that I move over to second base. And that's where I played for the rest of the season.

The way my baseball life turned out, I wish Sam had said, "You know what, Spring? Shut up. You're playing shortstop."

You see, I didn't realize at the time that in the minor leagues, it's about developing, not about winning. I didn't understand that if you're going to be a utility man in the big leagues, then you need to be able to play shortstop. If I had stayed the course in Jackson at the SS position, I believe I could have had a ten-year career in the majors as a utility guy. Especially the way I hit left-handed pitching. I felt I was cheating against lefties because their curve balls came right into my hitting zone. I could have given left-handed-hitting infielders a day off against lefties or maybe I could have been a platoon player.

It's amazing how things that don't seem important at the time can turn out to be huge.

A SIDE TRIP

While I was playing in the state of Mississippi, my brother, Gary, was playing for a team the next state over in Birmingham, Alabama, where he was the starting shortstop for the Birmingham Barons.

The Barons are the answer to a trivia question: *What minor league baseball team did basketball great Michael Jordan play for?* Jordan would play in Birmingham ten years after Gary's season with the Barons, batting .202 and deciding he should stick to basketball.

My brother had this to say:

GARY: Remember how I said I hated sharing a bedroom with Steve when we grew up? I was a neatness guy, and Steve . . . let's just say he was allergic to hangers and hampers.

The year he played in Jackson, I was playing for the Birmingham Barons. Even though Steve and I were only 240 miles apart, we were in separate leagues—I was in the Southern League and Steve was in the Texas League—so we never played against each other. We didn't make the playoffs, but the Jackson Mets did. When my season was over, I had to drive right through Jackson on Interstate 20 on my way to California, so naturally I wanted to see Steve play. Then we could drive home together once the playoffs were over.

Steve was sharing an apartment with several players. I knew that neatness and my brother were not well acquainted, but even this level of messiness was major league. When I walked into his bedroom, with dirty clothes thrown everywhere, the top three drawers in his dresser were pulled out in accordion-type fashion: the top drawer was pulled out four inches; the second drawer was pulled out eight inches; and the third drawer was pulled out a foot.

He hung clean shirts on the corners of each drawer because he was too lazy to put them on hangers and hang them up in his closet, which leads me to say this: For as long as I've known my brother, I can't recall him being passionate about anything except for baseball. If it wasn't for baseball, I don't know what Steve would be doing today.

Gary was right—I couldn't get my act together when it came to picking up after myself. To me, life was all about baseball and playing for the Jackson Mets, who were the class of our league. We finished with an 80-56 record in 1984 to propel us into the playoffs against the Wichita Aeros, who were affiliated with the San Diego Padres. We took the series 4-2, and I got my first championship ring in the minor leagues.

Our star player was left-handed outfielder Lenny Dykstra, nicknamed "Nails," who seemed to get all the attention. There's no doubt he had a good year. He batted .275, but I was right behind him at .273, so there wasn't much of a difference. The one tool that Lenny had over me was his speed. He stole 53 bases, and I had only six steals. Lenny committed just two errors in the outfield while I coughed up 23 errors in the infield.

When the season was over, I went back to the Instructional League for six weeks in September through October. For some reason, I caught the eye of Bob Schaefer, who was the manager of the Tidewater Tides, the Mets Triple-A team. Obviously, I wanted to do anything I could to impress him since I had my sights on a promotion to Triple-A.

When Instruction ball was finishing up, farm director Steve

Schryver told me about an opportunity to go right into "winter ball" in Colombia during the off-season. He wasn't talking about Columbia, South Carolina. Steve was describing the country of Colombia in South America. The country of drug trafficking and a perpetual civil war between the Revolutionary Armed Forces of Colombia (FARC), drug cartels, paramilitary groups, and the federal government.

Then again, I didn't pay attention to the news or remember what I learned about Colombia in some long-forgotten geography class. All I knew was that Colombia was a long way down there somewhere in South America.

I was up for an adventure, so I said yes and played for the Tigres de Cartagena. Even though my Spanish was limited to menu items like tacos and quesadillas, even I knew that Tigres meant "Tigers." The team was situated in Cartagena, a maritime port on the northern coast of Colombia in the Caribbean region. We were right on the beach.

Remember, this was 1984, so things were . . . *primitivo.* The food sucked. We were housed next to a Hilton Hotel, and the only American thing they had on the menu was spaghetti, so I ended up eating pasta and tomato sauce every single day I was in Colombia.

And wouldn't you know it: I roomed with Pete Kendrick, the pitcher from Brigham Young. He was the greatest guy and didn't mind me telling the world that I was 7-for-7 lifetime against him. We used to body surf every afternoon before we had to go to the ballpark. The tubular waves were outrageous—five or six feet in height—and the clear blue water was an unbelievable 85 degrees every day. It was a tropical paradise.

I played shortstop in Colombia. I did okay in the field but better in the hitting department, which was starting to become the story of my baseball life.

LOOKING AHEAD

I only got a couple of weeks off between the end of winter ball in Colombia and the start of spring training. At the time, I didn't mind. In the spring of 1985, I was twenty-four years old, at the height of my physical prime.

I wondered if I could get called up to Triple-A. I only hit five home runs in Jackson, which was a drop-off in production from my year in Columbia, when I had 12 four-baggers. Going into the last day of spring training, I still didn't know where I was going to play.

John Cumberland, the pitching coach for the Tidewater team, later told me that manager Bob Schaefer had walked into a meeting of the Mets farm executives and announced, "Springer is going to be my second baseman. Now let's move on."

There were looks exchanged around the table—looks that said, *Shafe, you're an idiot. Sure, take him. You got him.*

Joining me in Norfolk, Virginia, were Lenny Dykstra and Billy Beane, who became my roommates. I started off the season 16 for 100. I was brutal. That's a batting average of .160, far under the infamous "Mendoza line" of .200, which is typically defined as the threshold of incompetent hitting.

One time after another poor outing, I sat next to Shafe on a plane. (In Triple-A, you generally fly on road trips, compared to long bus rides in Double-A and Single-A.)

"Spring, they want to send you down to Double-A," he said.

"That sucks," I said.

Schaefer patted me on the knee. "You're not going anywhere. I told them you're hitting the crap out of the ball. You're just not getting the hits, I told them."

Hearing Shafe say that inspired me. Just knowing that he went to bat for me at a time when I couldn't buy a hit pumped me up.

I stayed in Norfolk and hit way over .300 the rest of the season, lifting my batting average to .261 at season's end. The 1985 season turned out not to be a disaster after all.

This was the first of four seasons with the Tidewater Mets. Think about it: I was one rung below the major leagues and knew I could be called up at any time, but the Mets were really good—and one of baseball's best teams in the mid-1980s. With players like catcher Gary Carter, outfielders George Foster, Mookie Wilson, and Daryl Strawberry, first baseman Keith Hernandez, and pitcher Dwight Gooden, the Mets won 98 games in 1985 but didn't get to the playoffs. In those days, only the divisional winners advanced, and the St. Louis Cardinals won 101 games in the National League East.

The following season, the Mets fashioned a franchise-best 108-54 record and played the Boston Red Sox in one of the most famous World Series games in baseball history—Game 6. Down 3-2 in the series, the Mets were down to their last pitch in the bottom of the tenth inning but fought back to tie the score. With Ray Knight on second base, Mookie Wilson hit a slow rolling ground ball up the first base line toward Bill Buckner, the Red Sox left-handed first baseman known for having creaky ankles.

I was watching the game back home in Huntington Beach, surrounded by Dad, Mom, Gary, and several friends in our living room. Los Angeles Dodgers broadcaster Vin Scully was calling the game for NBC. I had grown up listening to Vinnie and can still remember his call:

> So the winning run is at second base, with two outs, three-and-two to Mookie Wilson . . . little roller up along first . . . *behind the bag! It gets through Buckner! Here comes Knight, and the Mets win it!*

Shea Stadium—and our living room—exploded when Buckner let the ball roll under his glove, allowing Ray Knight to round third base and score the winning run. I punched my fist in the air because I had a lot of friends up there in New York. I was definitely pulling for them, including Rich Aguilera, who got the win. Vinnie then remained silent for more than three minutes, letting the pictures and the crowd noise tell the story.

The Red Sox, who hadn't won the World Series since 1918, couldn't bounce back from one of the most absolute bizarre finishes to a baseball game ever. The Mets would win Game 7 and the World Series—and keep alive the "Curse of the Bambino," referring to the Red Sox' sale of home run king Babe Ruth to the New York Yankees in 1920.

In the 1987 season, the Mets, as reigning world champs, played great with a 92–70 record, but that was only good enough for second place in the National League East. St. Louis advanced to the National League Championship Series with a 95–67 record. Under the rules at the time, the Mets didn't qualify for the playoffs.

During this three-year run of great Mets teams, there was no place for me to go from Tidewater. I batted .273 and .281 in 1986 and 1987, respectively, and I really thought I had a chance to be called up when second baseman Tim Teufel got hurt midway through the 1987 season, as I described in Chapter 1. But it wasn't meant to be.

When the 1987 season was over, I thought the least the Mets could do was invite me to the big league camp for spring training. That didn't happen, which was telling. At twenty-six years of age, I was no longer a prospect. My brother Gary came to the same conclusion as well just before the 1988 season.

Gary, who'd recently married Kim—whom he'd met in Birmingham while playing there—hurt his back in spring training. He was part of the Kansas City Royals organization at the time, and the parent club wanted to send him back to Double-A. Then Kim learned she was pregnant, and the doctor instructed that she couldn't fly, so Gary wouldn't see her for six months.

At twenty-eight years of age, it was time for Gary to move on with life. He retired from baseball and started working with my dad for a short time, but then he started a carpet cleaning business with Mark Dapello.

As for me, I was still single. Even though the pay had gotten better, I was still making less than $20,000 a year. But I wasn't about to quit, not when I was so close. The problem for me is that I had nowhere to go in the Mets organization—and I had no leverage.

All I could do was keep plugging away.

Meet the Press

*M*idway through the 1988 season, a *Los Angeles Times* reporter, Mike DiGiovanna, called me from the West Coast. I had no idea how he got my name or the telephone number of my apartment, but he wanted to write a "local guy trying to get to the big leagues" type of story. DiGiovanna was a beat writer for the *Times*, covering major league baseball.

His feature article, which appeared in my hometown newspaper on July 6, 1988, pretty much nailed it—the ups, the downs, and the challenges that lay ahead. Because this *Los Angeles Times* story captured my mindset as well as summarized my time in the minor leagues up to that point, I thought it would be instructive to share this article with you. Here's the *Los Angeles Times* story, which is reprinted with permission, in its entirety:

SPRINGER IS JUST TREADING WATER IN TIDEWATER

by Mike DiGiovanna

NORFOLK, VA—Steve Springer's baseball career had been cruising along at a steady pace during his first four years in the New York Mets organization.

Every season, Springer, a former Marina High School and Golden West College infielder, moved up a notch in the farm system, going from rookie ball in 1982 to Class A in 1983, Double-A in 1984 and Triple-A in 1985. But ever since Springer reached Norfolk, home of the Triple-A Tidewater Tides, he has hit nothing but roadblocks.

This is his fourth and probably most frustrating season at Tidewater. Here he is, 27 years old with almost seven seasons of professional experience, and he has never played in the major leagues. Springer, a 6-foot, 190-pounder, has never been invited to a big league spring training camp. He has never been called up in September. He has never had that proverbial cup of coffee in the major leagues.

Heck, he hasn't even smelled the brew.

The closest Springer, who throws and hits right-handed, has come to Shea Stadium was being mentioned by Met broadcaster Tim McCarver as a possible roster replacement when Met second baseman Tim Teufel injured a hamstring in April.

"That's my claim to fame," Springer said.

Springer received several calls from friends in California who had tuned in to the telecast, but he never got the call from the Mets, and he does not appear to fit into their plans.

"I've never really felt like a prospect. That's the indication I've gotten here," Springer said. "They don't have any plans for me. I'm just helping them out in Triple-A."

Springer, who has played outfield, third base, shortstop and second base, has decent statistics at Tidewater. His batting average improved from .261 in 1985 to .273

in 1986 and .281 in 1987 before it dipped to .249 this season.

In three-and-a-half years of Triple-A, he has hit 19 home runs and 73 doubles and has 173 RBIs. He has fared well against left-handed pitchers but has had problems against right-handed, breaking-ball pitchers. He has struck out at least 72 times in each of the past three seasons, and 50 times this year.

"A .268 lifetime average at Tidewater isn't bad, and that's with some serious slumps in there," Springer said. "But to get to the big leagues, you need one of the tools, either speed or power. I only have a little of both."

It also hasn't helped that Springer is in one of baseball's best organizations—one that is loaded with good infielders.

The Mets have two quality second basemen, Teufel and Wally Backman. It appears that rookie Kevin Elster, who also went to Marina High and Golden West, will be the Mets' shortstop for years to come. Howard Johnson is the third baseman and can fill in at short.

On the bench, the Mets have versatile infielders Dave Magadan, who can play first or third, and speedy Keith Miller, who can play second, short or third. Miller has been shuttling between New York and Tidewater this season.

Springer's best position is third base, but he is playing second this season. Why? Because the next Met phenom, 20-year-old Gregg Jefferies, is playing third.

"I really feel that if I was with another organization last year, I would have been called up in September," said Springer, who was a 20th-round draft pick out of the University of Utah. "That's the bad thing about being with the Mets. They have so much talent."

Springer thinks he can be a utility man in the major leagues, and he has asked the Mets to trade him. But Steve Schryver, the Mets' director of minor league operations, said no major league teams have been interested.

"There would be no shortage of teams that would take Steve at Triple-A, but there's no benefit to a lateral move," Schryver said.

"There hasn't been any club that has expressed a desire to acquire his services at the major league level."

Is this discouraging to Springer?

"If they're telling the truth, it is," he said.

Mike Cubbage, the Tide manager, said he feels Springer could play major league baseball "in the right situation." Apparently, that situation isn't with New York.

But Springer is not ready to give up. He will be a free agent in two months and believes he can catch on with another major league team by next season.

"I look at it as a positive," Springer said. "I don't look at it as, 'Oh, shoot, I'm 27. I'm too old to make it.' Sure, I'm too old to make the Hall of Fame. But I've got a few good years left."

Springer, who is engaged to Teri Moore, 28, of Corona del Mar, doesn't plan to retire from baseball until he is released a few times, even if that means playing Triple-A ball again. He's earning top dollar for a minor leaguer—about $3,600 a month during the season, compared with the $2,000 a month most non-roster Triple-A players receive.

"As long as I stay healthy, I won't quit," he said. "There's too much money to be made up there, and I'm not that far away. I love baseball, and I want to coach when I'm done playing. I could always work for my dad, but I'd rather play."

Sure, I could work for Dad, who'd purchased the Carl Brooks company, but I really didn't want to put together sheet metal buildings for a living. I'd rather play baseball until the day no professional team wanted me.

Looking back, I wish I'd said this to DiGiovanna: "Given where I was in high school, I can't believe I've made it this far. Playing baseball for a living sure beats real work."

I was totally content being in Triple-A. I still dreamed of getting my shot, but if I needed a dose of encouragement, I recalled players on my Triple-A teams who got called up even though they weren't as good as me on the ball field. My mindset was this: *They're going to have to rip this jersey off of me more than once for me to quit baseball and get a real job.*

Sure, the money wasn't very good, but I could afford all the necessities. This didn't mean I didn't care whether I got to the major leagues. Far from it. Getting called up was still a burning desire in my heart. What I'm trying to say is that I never forgot where I came from, which was sitting on the bench in high school and junior college and coaching first base. I knew I had the patience and the grit to keep playing for as long as I could.

When the *Times* story came out, I was engaged to Teri. I met her six months earlier during the off-season when Joe Redfield and I went out to Hogue Barmichael's, a happening place in Newport Beach. When I spotted Teri for the first time, it was just like in the movies. She captured my eye. I had to introduce myself. After walking across the bar to where she was sitting, I delivered the best pick-up line I could muster. "You're the prettiest girl by far in this place," I said.

She accepted the compliment and smiled. "Why, thank you," she said.

I breathed a sigh of relief. She didn't tell me to take a hike.

"What's your name?" I asked.

"Teri," she said.

"My name is Steve."

No Dick Fox for me. I wasn't going to make my father's mistake.

We started talking. Turned out she was a waitress. I told her I played baseball for the New York Mets. Well, I fudged a bit there. Telling her I played for a minor league team in the New York Mets organization would have been more accurate, but I was playing for keeps here. After ten minutes of chitchat, I went for broke: "Can I take you out for dinner?"

Teri looked at me. "I don't even know you."

"Don't worry. I'm the nicest guy in the world. Just ask my mom."

Teri flashed another smile. She was warming up to me. She didn't agree to dinner that night, but she gave me her phone number, which I guarded like a $100 bill.

Two days later, we went out to the movies and dinner, and from then on, we were an item. We saw each other every day until I left for spring training in 1988.

I ended up back with the Tidewater Mets, playing second base. Teri and I continued a long-distance relationship. At some point, I asked her to marry me, and she said yes.

A month after the *Los Angeles Times* article came out, my baseball life took a new twist: I was traded to the Chicago White Sox, part of a four-man trade that sent me and pitcher Tom McCarthy to the White Sox in exchange for Vince Harris and Mike Maksudian.

In the locker room, this was known as a crap-for-crap trade, meaning both clubs were moving around players they viewed as dead wood. It wasn't like the White Sox really wanted me or I was going straight to the big leagues, although I liked busting the chops of my good friend Tom McCarthy, telling him, *Dude, you were a throw-in in that deal.*

I was optioned to the Vancouver Canadians, the White Sox' Triple-A club, for the last month of the season. From above the 49th parallel near the Canadian Rockies, the major leagues never looked further away. Desperate times called for desperate measures.

When the season was over, I let my coaches know that I was willing to give catching a try. They knew I had a bazooka for an arm, so they arranged for me to go to Florida for the fall Instructional

League, where I donned the "tools of ignorance"—the catcher's mask, chest protector, and shin guards. I hadn't been behind the plate since Little League, but once the league games started, it was like I had been a catcher all my life.

I threw out the first five guys trying to steal second because of my arm. The coaches told me I had great "transfer," meaning I got the ball out of the mitt quickly so I could make the long throw to second base on time.

But after Instructional ball, I decided that I didn't want to become an everyday catcher. With seven seasons of minor league baseball under my belt, it was too late to make the change. I told my coaches that I was willing to catch, but only if the team needed me in an emergency.

I set my sights on becoming a utility guy. If I could fill in at catcher and one of the infield positions, I would make myself more valuable to my team.

BOWLING THEM OVER

In February 1989, the White Sox invited me to take part in the big league spring training, which was a first for me. I'd always been stuck in the minor league side of spring training.

When I arrived in Sarasota, Florida, for camp, I was coached on the finer aspects of catching by future Hall of Famer Carlton Fisk and backups Mark Merillo and Ron Karkovice. I did wind up catching one game, and my knees were killing me afterward—a sign that I could never become a full-time catcher. The White Sox put me at third base, where I did fine, but I didn't expect to make the parent club.

One time, in the locker room after a spring training exhibition game, I overheard two Chicago White Sox players, Kenny Williams and Darryl Boston, talking about going bowling. (Today, Kenny is the Executive Vice President of the White Sox, and Darryl had a nice ten-year career in the big leagues.)

Hearing the word *bowling* perked up my ears. "You guys going bowling?" I asked.

Now, you have to understand the dynamics going on here. I was a scrub who hadn't made the team and they were big league studs, so there was a pecking order in play. Based on that status, Darryl good-naturedly teased me.

"You want some of this, you little Barney Rubble-looking sucker?" He razzed me pretty good.

"I think I do, buddy," I said.

They had no idea that I was practically raised in a bowling alley because my mom worked there, but I wasn't going to let them know that. There was some money to be won here.

So we went bowling, and it was like taking candy from baby twins. I rolled a 220 in the first game and collected a $20 bill from each of them.

"You wanna keep playing?" I asked.

Kenny and Darryl looked at each other. I'm sure they thought I was the luckiest bowler ever.

That night, I walked away from the bowling alley $120 richer. I had so much fun taking their money.

When spring training broke, I was shipped off to Vancouver. I sure wish hitting a baseball at Vancouver's Nat Bailey Stadium—"The Nat"—was easier than winning bowling bets. In Rain City, the ball didn't carry in the damp atmosphere. Nonetheless, I still played well. I batted .277 with eight home runs and was voted the Most Valuable Player on the team. Better yet, I helped our team win the Pacific Coast League championship for my second ring.

Did I get a September call-up?

Nope. The White Sox elevated a twenty-one-year-old third baseman from Double-A named Robin Ventura. I guess the White Sox knew what they were doing: Ventura ended up playing sixteen seasons in the major leagues before going into managing, where he was the skipper of the White Sox from 2012 to 2016.

I was bummed to be passed over once again. Would I ever get a chance to play for a major league ball club? I was really starting to wonder.

After the 1989 season, I was declared a minor league free agent since I had played six full seasons in the minors. I could now choose who I wanted to play for—as long as that team wanted me to play for them.

During the off-season, my agent made a few phone calls on my behalf. The Seattle Mariners and Cleveland Indians expressed an interest in signing me. I thought I was a better match with the Indians. I was happy to learn that I was invited to the big league camp for spring training.

Just before I left for spring training in Phoenix, Teri and I were on the rocks. Our engagement was off. I told Joe Redfield that if I ever got back together with her, then he had my permission to slap the crap out of me.

Three weeks later, we got married—and twenty-seven years and two children later, I'm glad we did. Since I had to get to spring training, we couldn't take an official honeymoon. (Teri says we still haven't taken one.) We packed up my Honda Accord and drove across the California desert to Phoenix. Once again, I didn't make the twenty-five-man roster.

I knew the drill. I was going to Triple-A.

That night, when I told Teri the news, her first question was, "Where are we going?"

"Colorado Springs," I replied.

"Where's that?"

"I'm not sure."

Like Teri, I knew Colorado Springs was somewhere in Colorado, but I wasn't sure exactly where the city was located in the Rocky Mountain State.

Something told me that this would be my last chance to make it to the major leagues.

13

Hearing the Call

The Cleveland Indians farm director, Johnny Goura, shifted in his seat inside the manager's office. We were at home in Colorado Springs, playing the Tucson Toros in a three-game series. The Colorado Springs Sky Sox were six weeks into the 1990 season, and I was Mr. Steady, batting in the .270s and splitting my time between second base and third base.

Normally, when your team manager asks you to come to his office and you see the farm director sitting there, it means one of four things:

- you're going up
- you're going down
- you've been traded
- you've been released

I didn't think I was being called up. After being so close on many occasions—only to experience the sting of disappointment—I had mentally walled off the possibility of playing in the major leagues.

In my mind, I didn't want to go there or be obsessed about making it to the majors. If it happened, great. If not, then that was my fate.

Like Hack had told me around the batting cage in Colorado Springs, I had a label as a Triple-A guy. Even though I didn't want to believe I was stuck in the minors—I'd always been a "glass is half full" type of guy—the thought occurred to me that after playing more than 1,000 games of Triple-A ball, perhaps I had hit a glass ceiling. It was looking like the major leagues would always be a little bit out of reach.

I didn't think I was being sent down to Double-A. At twenty-nine years of age, I was too old to play in a league populated with twenty-one-, twenty-two-, and twenty-three-year-old players fresh from college. So going to Double-A was out.

As for whether I had been traded, that was a possibility. Being shipped to the White Sox two years earlier had been out of the blue, but given my age—I was considered "old" in baseball years—I didn't think another organization would want a twenty-nine-year-old player who'd never been in The Show.

So Johnny Goura's presence could only mean one thing: I was being released for acting like an idiot the previous night, when I'd angrily flung my bat across the dugout and said a few swear words after my manager, Bobby Molinaro, pinch-hit for me in the middle of an at-bat—in a game in which I hit a home run!

I'd seen the axe fall a zillion times over the years for far less. Baseball was a brutal sport in that regard. You're here today and gone tomorrow. Players could be released at any time, even in mid-May.

So this could be the end of the line. I maintained a poker face because there was another thing I'd learned over the years: You never know what will happen in professional baseball.

A smile creased Goura's lips.

"Spring, you're going to the big leagues."

Did I hear right? Or was this another trick, like Lucy pulling away the football just as Charlie Brown was about to kick?

"Really?" I wanted to be sure.

"Yup, your day has come," Goura said. "You're being called up."

My body went numb. Time came to a standstill. My mind blanked for a moment as the significance of realizing a childhood dream washed over me. The feeling of sheer happiness was overwhelming. I bowed my head and whispered a prayer.

Thank you, Jesus.

And that's when I allowed the joy of the moment to settle in my heart.

"This is great news!" I exclaimed. "I can't believe this is happening. I really can't."

Johnny Goura and Bobby Molinaro exchanged knowing glances. They had witnessed this type of response dozens of times, and I imagined that it never got old.

"So what happens next?" I asked.

"You'll drive up to Stapleton tomorrow morning and take the first flight to Cleveland," Goura said, referring to the Denver airport. "The team is starting a week-long homestand, so good timing."

I knew that players getting called-up mid-season sometimes came right back down. As if he was reading my mind, Goura said, "We don't know how long you'll be in Cleveland, so don't get an apartment."

"Understood," I said.

"Go home and pack," Goura continued. "I'll have the travel secretary contact you about your travel arrangements."

I stood and shook Goura's hand, thanking him for the opportunity to play in the big leagues. The next thing I did was call Teri with the good news. She erupted in delight, followed by a million questions: *When are you going? How do I get to Cleveland? How will I find you?*

I told her that since no one knew how long I would be with the Indians, the team put up players and their wives in a downtown

Cleveland hotel until things got sorted out.

My next phone call was to Huntington Beach. It was the weekend, so Dad picked up at the house on Mar Vista. I don't think he believed me at first, even though he knew I wouldn't joke about being called up if it didn't happen. Nonetheless, he was still caught off-guard.

"You're not messing with me, are you?" he said sternly.

"No, Dad. I wouldn't do that. You're going to be the father of a son who plays in the major leagues."

Mom and Cori got on the line, too. Cori was entering high school, and she and Mom had watched me play in dozens of games over the years. They were overjoyed to hear the good news also. Everyone was pumped, including Gary the Great, who was as excited as I was when I reached him.

My older brother and I had a special bond, and there was no way I could have played pro baseball, yet alone finally get a call-up to the big leagues, without him in my life. The years of battling each other drove me to become the competitor that I was on the field. I actually had the feeling that I was going to the major leagues for the both of us.

"I'll be your way at the end of the month," I told Gary.

One of the first things I did after getting called up was to check the Indians' schedule to see when the team came through Anaheim. The Indians played in the American League East Division, and the California Angels were in the AL West Division, so the Indians only made two West Coast swings during the season. I caught a break when I learned that we'd be playing in my hometown in a couple of weeks.

Mom got back on the line. "Be sure to get plenty of tickets," she said. "We all want to see you play in a major league game."

"That would be cool, Mom. Very cool."

IN CLEVELAND

I always heard it said that the difference between the major leagues and the minor leagues was like night and day.

They were right.

I'll start with what you see. I noticed right away how the players were catered to in every way and treated deferentially. The whole major league scene was larger than life: the stadiums, the locker rooms, and the number of personnel on hand to take care of the ballplayers. There were plenty of trainers to tape you up and work out any muscular kinks with deep-tissue massage.

The food set out for the players—known as "The Spread"—was amazing. No more tubs of peanut butter and jelly to make your own Wonder Bread sandwiches. There was an array of expensive foods set out on a couple of tables: barbecued steak, shrimp kabobs, fried chicken, two types of pasta, fresh salads, and yummy desserts. The per diem—cash given to players to pay for restaurant meals while on the road—was $80 a day. That sure beat the $18 a day in Triple-A that got spent on McDonald's. (Then again, I always had a fondness for McDonald's hamburgers, no pickles, no onions.)

And then there was the salary bump. I was one of the highest-paid players in Triple-A because of my length of service, earning about $6,000 a month during the season, which worked out to around $30,000 (or $55,000 in today's dollars) in a season. But once I reached the big leagues, I started receiving the major league minimum, which was $100,000 in 1990 (or $182,700 in today's dollars). That meant my bi-monthly paycheck more than tripled. I was thrilled.

Inside the white lines, the difference was not that dramatic. While I was in the minors, I played with and against many former major leaguers over the years, so I knew firsthand that minor league players could play baseball as well as major league players. We just needed to be a tick more consistent.

That said, the major leagues are another level because statistics don't lie. Hitters are remembered—and paid accordingly—for their batting average, number of hits, doubles, triples, home runs, bases on balls, intentional walks, stolen bases, and runs batted in. Pitchers are judged by their win-loss records, earned run averages, strikeouts, walks, and innings pitched, to name a few measurements.

When I arrived in Cleveland, I took it all in from a seat on the bench. I loved every minute I wore a big league uniform, donning No. 2 for the Indians. As the first few games of the home stand passed by, however, I was understandably itchy to play. I didn't work all those years to get to a major league dugout only to never get in a game, did I? I heard stories of that happening to players who were on major league teams but never got to play.

I did my best to be ready, arriving in plenty of time to take batting and fielding practice. I was Johnny Hustle on the diamond but cool and relaxed at the same time. I didn't want to blow this opportunity.

The California Angels were in Cleveland for a two-game series, which raised my comfort level. I had grown up with the Halos and their navy blue and red accents on gray road uniforms. After losing the first game of the series, our manager, John McNamara, dropped by my locker.

"Spring, you're playing tomorrow night. I'm starting you at third base," he said.

I stood up to thank him. "Thanks, Mac" I said. "I can't wait."

Mac had a word of advice for me. "Don't turn white on me," he said, meaning don't get freaked out. He knew as well as I did what it took to get here—and how much playing in the major leagues meant to me.

I'll never forget May 22, 1990, the date I became the 13,369th player in Major League Baseball history. I'll always remember seeing the lineup card posted in the clubhouse before the game, where **Springer 3B** was handwritten in the ninth slot. Seeing that lineup card gave me the chills.

Of course I didn't mind that I was batting last in the lineup. (Remember, this is the American League, where a designated hitter is allowed to bat for the pitcher.) I was immensely happy to get a major league start.

I'd heard the National Anthem played a couple of thousand times before a ballgame, but it was like I was hearing this stirring song for the first time as I stood near third base with my Indians hat over my chest. I had a few moments to drink it all in, and then flashbacks occurred . . . high school coaches telling me *You're too small* or *You'll never play* . . . college coaches saying, *You're not ready yet* . . . *go coach first base*. All these images came into my mind.

I shot a quick glance to the field level seats. Teri was sitting by herself in the Indians family section because she didn't feel comfortable enough to introduce herself to any of the player wives. I hadn't played yet. I wasn't part of the club.

But that was all about to change.

The first couple of innings passed by without incident. I didn't get to bat until the bottom of the third inning. Chuck Finley, a tall and rangy left-hander, was on the mound for the Angels. Known as a power pitcher, Finley was among the league leaders in strikeouts with a heavy fastball and devastating forkball.

As I took a knee in the on deck circle, I couldn't believe how quiet it was in Cleveland Stadium, an old school ballpark that opened in 1931 with 75,000 seats. Not many fans had turned out for the Tuesday night game. Just one-tenth of the seats were filled—the attendance was 7,333 that night.

I'll admit that my heart was beating extra fast when it came time for me to approach the plate for my first big league at-bat. Finley undoubtedly did his homework before the game and knew that the No. 9 batter was making his major league debut. I figured he'd start me off with a fastball, his money pitch.

Sure enough, Finley threw me a first-pitch fastball. I was ready. I swung and hit an absolute missile to right-center. It looked like a double the entire way. I was halfway down the first base line when I glanced up. Dave Winfield, a 6-foot, 6-inch right fielder—a future Hall of Famer and seven-time Gold Glove Award winner—took five giant steps and snatched the liner at his feet.

A shoestring catch.

I was bummed, but I wasn't going to hang my head.

When I came up in the bottom of the sixth, I got a curveball to start the at-bat. I let that one go by for a called strike. Finley's second pitch was a fastball outside.

With a 1-1 count, Finley threw me split-finger fastball. I swung and broke my bat; I like to joke that my knuckles are still in Cleveland. I hit a little flair over the outstretched glove of second baseman Johnny Ray and into right field for my first big league hit.

I was ecstatic! No one was on base at the time, but I noticed that instead of the ball being returned to the pitcher, the ball was tossed toward our dugout for safekeeping. I have that souvenir baseball today.

"Nice job," said the first baseman. "I remember you from Utah."

"Thanks, Wally."

Wally Joyner, the Brigham Young star, was the Angels first baseman.

In the bottom of sixth, with a 4-0 deficit, we mounted a three-run rally. When the Angels brought in a right-handed reliever, Bryan Harvey, Mac pinch-hit left-handed hitter Dion James for me. I was done for the night.

The game, which we ended up losing 8-3, wasn't broadcast on national TV, so there was no way for my family to watch the game in those pre-Internet days. They were ecstatic when I called from the clubhouse after the game. I was 1-for-2 in my first game, which made me a lifetime .500 hitter in the major leagues!

There wasn't much time to celebrate. I hugged Teri outside the locker room and then the team boarded a bus for our charter flight to Seattle. The following night, we were to play the Mariners as part of a West Coast swing that would also take us to Oakland and Anaheim against the Angels. We decided that Teri would fly out to Orange County and wait for me there.

NORTHWEST PASSAGE

*M*ac gave me another start two days later in the Seattle Kingdome. I'd never played indoors before, so the lighting and sounds were all different but I adjusted. Batting ninth again, I went 1-for-4 with a single in a 5-3 victory.

The following night, I got another start in Oakland and a "promotion" to eighth in the batting order. I went 0-for-2 but in my second at-bat, I got my first major league run batted in with a sacrifice fly. Home runs by the "Bash Brothers"—Mark McGwire and Jose Canseco—sunk us, however.

I'll admit that I was looking ahead to the last stop on the road trip—a three-game set against the California Angels. I was so excited that I was like a kid on Christmas morning. Everyone was going to be there—my family, my neighborhood friends growing up, and my old classmates. I had fifty names on my "comp" list, so I had to scramble to get enough tickets.

Mac knew I was from Orange County. I looked at the pitching

matchups and saw that we would be facing two left-handers—Jim Abbott and Mark Langston. I figured I'd play at least once in front of family and friends.

I wasn't in the lineup for the first game of the series against Abbott. I was bummed, but I wasn't going to let it get me down. Then, just before the first pitch, I saw my buddy-since-childhood Matt Blaty walking up to home plate to sing the National Anthem. (It turns out that Matt, who stayed at Disneyland and made it a career, moonlighted as a singer of the National Anthem at Dodgers, Angels, Lakers, Clippers, and Kings games.)

I'm told that Dad wiped away tears as Matt sang *O say can you see, by the dawn's early light* . . . in perfect pitch.

Who would have thought that two little kids who grew up as best friends would end up at Angels Stadium, one wearing a major league uniform and the other singing the National Anthem before the game? I warned Matt before the game that the players don't like long, drawn-out anthems since they hear the song every day. My longtime friend didn't let me down. He sung the quickest and best anthem of the year, according to my teammates.

We returned to Cleveland for a series with the Boston Red Sox. I was still sitting when Roger Clemons took the mound with an 8-2 record. In 1990, Clemons was the best pitcher in baseball and in the prime of his pitching career, a hard thrower with a great command of his pitches.

In the bottom of the first, our leadoff hitter Stan Jefferson was hit with the second pitch of the game. It was a "message pitch" and retaliation for a brushback delivery thrown by one of our pitchers the previous night at Tony Pena of the Red Sox.

Both benches emptied, and another baseball brawl ensued. I joined the fracas and pushed some players around, but no punches were thrown. Our third baseman that night, Chris James, was ejected, however.

Mac found me on the bench. "You're in," he barked.

Suddenly I was batting fifth against Roger Clemons. Later, in the bottom of the first, we had runners on second and third, two outs. Clemons threw me a 2-2 inside fastball. I hit the hardest ball I would ever hit in the big leagues in the 5-6 hole between third and short. Luis Rivera, the Red Sox shortstop, leaped and snagged the liner with full extension for the inning-ending out, saving his team two runs.

Clemons was a smart pitcher. The rest of the night, he didn't throw me another fastball for a strike. Instead, he fed a steady diet of splitties—split-fingered fastballs—that looked like fastballs but suddenly "dropped off the table" when they arrived at home plate. I struck out three times. He even threw me a 3-2 slider with a 7-2 lead with two outs and a runner on second. By then I was sort of looking for it, but I still swung and missed.

Three days later, I was in the clubhouse before the game. I looked up and saw Jeff Manto, a teammate from Colorado Springs. He was a first baseman who also played some third base.

"Nice, dude. I see they called you up," I said.

"Yeah, it's great to be here." Jeff beamed. It was his first time in the big leagues, so I understood the wide smile.

One of the coaches came by my locker. "Mac wants to see you in his office," he said.

Uh-oh. That's usually not good news.

"Spring, we got our wires crossed. Sorry about this, but they're sending you down to Colorado Springs," John McNamara said.

After three weeks in the big leagues, I had to pack up and go.

I didn't know if I would ever get back.

14

Back for a Cup of Coffee

*A*fter Keith Miller, my teammate on the Tidewater Tides, got called up instead of me in 1987, I asked him what it was like being in the big leagues.

"Spring, picture it as good as you can picture it, and then times it by ten," he said.

I had heard a hundred players echo the same words over the years. Now I knew what they meant. Everything was bigger in the major leagues—the crowds, the atmosphere, and the attention on the ballplayers.

Back in Colorado Springs, I continued to play well, leading the team in doubles and maintaining a batting average in the .270s. Then something strange happened the first week of August: the opposing team started a left-handed pitcher, and I wasn't in the lineup.

That didn't make sense. I *always* hit left-handed pitching well. It was the curve ball from right-handers that gave me fits—and probably kept me from playing many years in the major leagues.

I sought out our manager, Charlie Manuel, before the game.

Bobby Molinaro had been fired mid-season because the organization thought they needed to make a change. His antics got old.

"Charlie, what am I now? A utility guy who gets a spot start every now and then?"

Charlie looked up from the paperwork. "Spring, it's worse than that. I gotta release you after the game."

Did I hear right? I was being handed my walking papers? A cold shiver traveled down my spine.

"Why am I being released? I'm one of the best hitters on the team."

Charlie looked pained. "Yeah, I know it doesn't make sense, but I have my orders."

I later learned that I was let go as a cost-cutting move by the Indians, but someone in the front office didn't realize that since I had played in the big leagues back in May, the team had to pay my minor league salary through the end of September. In other words, there was no savings to the team.

As soon as my release was official, my agent got a call from the San Diego Padres. They wanted me for their Triple-A team in Las Vegas, and they wanted me *now*.

Turns out I was out of a job for ten minutes. Teri and I packed up our belongings, loaded the van, and started the daylong drive to Vegas. When we arrived, I learned even more good news: the Padres were going to pay me $3,000 a month while the Indians continued forking over $6,000 a month. That meant I was knocking down $9,000 a month—tall cotton for someone playing in the minor leagues.

After the 1990 season, when I experienced the highest of highs and the lowest of lows, I was a six-year free agent again, eligible to sign with any team. The Seattle Mariners picked me up for the 1991 campaign. They sent me to their Triple-A affiliate in Calgary, Canada, where I batted .257 for the Cannons and hit 17 home runs—a big power surge for me.

Once again, I was a free agent at the end of the season. My old team—the New York Mets—wanted me, so I was still in baseball. Better yet, I returned to a place where I felt quite comfortable: Norfolk, Virginia, home of the Tidewater Tides. I was also reunited with two great coaches that I loved: manager Clint Hurdle and bench coach Ron Washington.

In mid-August, I was batting in the .290s—a career high at age thirty-one!—with 16 home runs. Wash came by my locker. "Clint wants to see you," he said.

I followed Wash into Clint's office, and it was like a love fest. "Spring, we got great news for you," said my manager. "You've been called up."

I don't know who was happier—my coaches or me. They knew how long I had been grinding. Now I was back in the big leagues with the Mets!

One of the first Mets players I saw in the Shea Stadium locker room was pitcher Dwight Gooden. Nicknamed "Dr. K," Doc was the ace of the Mets staff and a Cy Young award winner. I knew Doc before he was Doc. We had played together in Little Falls following the 1982 Major League Draft. I was a 21-year-old nobody coming out of Utah while Dwight was a seventeen-year-old phenom drafted out of high school in the first round—the fifth player taken.

I remember shagging balls in the outfield one afternoon in Little Falls. Dwight and I clicked right away, and I loved teasing him. On this occasion, I ribbed him by saying, "Man, you ain't five hundred picks better than me."

Just then, a lazy fly ball came in our direction, which Dwight easily snatched out of the sky. "Trust me, Spring. I am," he said.

I guess he had a point.

This time I didn't have to wait long to get my first National

League appearance. A day after I caught up with the team, I pinch-hit against Mitch "Wild Thing" Williams of the Philadelphia Phillies. True to his nickname, if I didn't swing at a couple of bad pitches, I walked. Instead, I struck out on pitches outside the strike zone.

Then we embarked on a West Coast swing that started in Los Angeles. Once again, I was really excited to be wearing a major league uniform near my hometown. My parents, brother Gary, and my sisters, along with a lot of good friends, braved the traffic to be there at Dodgers Stadium. First game, I didn't play. Second game, I sat on the bench. Same for the final game of the series.

I must have dug a trench in the visitors' dugout from all the pacing I did. While we were batting in the top of the ninth—we were way ahead, 11-4—manager Jeff Torborg made eye contact with me.

His face brightened, like a light bulb went off.

"Oh, yeah," he said. "You're from here, right?"

"Yeah," I said. *And my family has never seen me play in a major league game.*

"Take third," he said.

Although I didn't get an at-bat, I did play a half-inning of defense. I'm told that Vin Scully, the legendary Dodgers announcer, mentioned my name.

We moved on to San Diego, where my parents and siblings *did* get to see me at the plate. I pinch-hit against Padres reliever Randy Myer but grounded out. That made me 0-for-2 and still looking for my first hit in the National League.

We moved on to San Francisco for a three-game series against the Giants. I didn't play the first game, which we won, but I noticed that Trevor Wilson, a lefty, was on the mound the next day. When the game was over, I joined my teammates for the walk from the dugout to the visitor's clubhouse, which was in right field. I spotted our manager Jeff Torborg alone in foul territory.

I hustled up alongside him. "Hey, for the record, the guy who's pitching tomorrow night, I took him deep in Triple-A," I said. "I can hit Wilson."

I wanted to put that thought in Torborg's mind since I hadn't gotten a start in the nine days I'd been called up.

Torborg accepted my "suggestion" and started me at second base the next night. The game was broadcast nationally on CBS with Sean McDonough and Tim McCarver in the booth. I called home before the game with the exciting news, so everyone was watching.

In the top of the second, batting seventh, I came up with a man on first and one out. I lined a double down the right field line, moving Kevin Bass to third. Then he scored on a wild pitch, giving the Mets a 1-0 lead.

I played well in the field and got another hit, a single, going 2-for-3 in a 2-1 win. I was even interviewed after the game on national TV! Back in the clubhouse, I was told that manager Jeff Torborg wanted to see me right away. I hadn't had time to even put my hat in the locker.

"You're being sent down," he said. "We need a pitcher. You'll be back in a week when we can expand the rosters."

After September 1, teams are allowed to increase their rosters to forty players.

Okay, I could handle that. The Mets were having a bad year and neck-and-neck for the basement of the National League East with the Phillies, so it wasn't like I could mess things up more than they were already.

Then my world was turned upside down two days later when the Mets traded pitcher David Cone to Toronto for Ryan Thompson and some stiff named Jeff Kent, who'd only go on to become the National League MVP in 2000 while setting the all-time record for home runs hit by a second baseman. At the time of the trade, Kent was in his rookie year at Toronto and not getting much playing time because future Hall of Famer Roberto Alomar was camped at second base.

So there went my call-up. Jeff Kent took my parking spot.

At season's end in Norfolk, I received the MVP award for my .290 average, 16 home runs, and 70 RBIs, by far my best season at an "advanced age" in baseball. Ironically, I had to make one more trip to New York, where I—along with all the other team MVPs in the Mets' farm system—were honored before a game. We each received a Doubleday Award.

I returned to the Tidewater Tides for the 1993 season. I hurt my back at the start of spring training so badly that I landed in the hospital for a week. I couldn't lift my butt out of bed.

Three weeks later, I rejoined the team. I could hit but couldn't bend over to field a ground ball to save my life. Clint brought me along slowly. I wore a back brace and really wasn't my old self until May or so.

In mid-season, when I felt 100 percent, I flippantly asked Clint, "When am I going to get one of those 'you're kidding me' call-ups?"

That's a baseball term for a call-up where everyone looks in the newspaper the following morning and says to himself, *You have to be kidding me—I'm better than him.*

Clint laughed. "Yeah, whatever," he said.

Two days later, he called me into his office following a night game.

"You're kidding me," he said.

My face brightened. "You mean I'm going up?"

"Yeah. The Mets want you in Montreal."

I returned to the locker room, sharing the good news and high-fiving teammates. I packed up my belongings and was about to leave for the airport when Clint pulled me into his office.

"Hey, something happened," he said. "Tonight, we were down three runs in Montreal, but Hundley hit a three-run blast that took the game into extra innings," he said, referring to Mets catcher Todd Hundley. "We played four more innings and used four more pitchers. Now the team needs another arm."

"You mean—"

"Yeah, they banged the promotion. Sorry about that."

I would never get called up again.

NEXT STOP

That was really my last opportunity to play in the major leagues even though I ended up playing two more seasons in Triple-A.

Sure, I was one of the oldest players in baseball's highest minor league level. I imagine that many of the players ten, twelve years younger than me were thinking, *How can you spend ten years in Triple-A?* Well, I had a job because I had some of my most productive hitting seasons in my career after I turned thirty.

In the early '90s, Triple-A ball wasn't all that bad. We flew commercially, so long, steamy bus rides were a thing of the past. We didn't bunk four-to-a-room in cheap motor inns but stayed in fairly decent hotels, each player in his own room. We didn't play in creaky old stadiums for the most part. During my last year with the Tides, we played in a brand-new $15 million, 12,000-seat stadium.

Salaries had risen as well. I was making $40,000 a year at the end of my career. That was enough to live on, even with a growing family. I always said things could have been a lot worse. I was doing something I loved to do, playing a game I loved. I made a zillion friends and was a leader in the clubhouse. There weren't a lot of jobs that paid you to sleep until 11 a.m. with five months off a year, which gave me plenty of time to work on my golf game during the off-season.

After the 1995 season, I was thirty-four years old. I was talking with my buddy Louie Medina, a former teammate at Colorado Springs who'd just gotten a job as a scout with the Arizona Diamondbacks.

"Dude, your playing career is killing your scouting career," he said.

As a student of the game, I had been thinking about getting into scouting.

Then Louie said, "We have an opening for an area scout in Orange County and San Diego, and I think you'd be perfect for it."

Since I didn't have much else going, a scouting gig sounded good to me—especially one that allowed us to settle down in Huntington Beach. After talking things through with Teri, I decided to retire and scout for the D-backs. After 1,591 games and 1,591 base hits in fourteen seasons of professional baseball—I was really glad to see that I averaged *exactly* one hit a game over the course of my career—it was time to do something else.

I was an area scout for two years with the Diamondbacks and then the West Coast cross-checker for three years, meaning I supervised five area scouts and would take a second look at the players they liked and rank them accordingly.

My scouting director was Don Mitchell, who liked me. He ended up quitting scouting and becoming a baseball agent. He knew what a good talker I was and thought I would be a natural baseball agent, so I quit scouting and joined his agency.

Jerry Maguire had nothing on me in the living room. I could talk young players and their parents into signing up with us for representation in no time at all.

I also saw the need to help these prospects. No matter what position they played, every young player wanted to be a better hitter. So did I when I was their age.

I thought about how I could best help my young prospects. And then I remembered something that happened when I was twenty-seven years old and playing for the Tidewater Tides. This circumstance happened before I reached the major leagues.

A roving instructor for the Mets dropped by Norfolk. His name was Tommy McCraw. He played thirteen seasons in the big leagues in the 1960s and '70s with five different teams and retired with a lifetime batting average of .246. Tommy was a pretty good player who got the most out of his ability.

Tommy was a born coach and a fountain of baseball wisdom, especially on the mental side of hitting. Every time Tommy passed through and shared his swing thoughts, I was good. I had strong at-bats and played with confidence.

And then Tommy would leave for the next town, and like the idiot I was, I'd go back to my old habits—swinging at bad pitches, not striding toward the pitcher, pulling my head off the baseball, and flying open with the front shoulder. Looking for everything and not ready for anything. Trying to hit everything thrown my way.

But as dumb as I was, I was smart enough to know that when Tommy was around, I hit well. So one day in 1987, I went to his hotel room with a tape recorder in hand.

"Tommy, could I record you on how I can become a better hitter?"

"Absolutely," Tommy said. "Get your butt in here." He saw how much this meant to me.

For the next twenty minutes, while my recorder whirled, he spoke about what batters needed to do to become better hitters.

"Spring, when does hitting start for you?" he began.

"When I'm in the on deck circle. That's when I take a look at the pitcher and see what kind of stuff he has."

"Actually, hitting starts when you pick up the newspaper in

the morning and check out who's pitching. That's when you start visualizing yourself hitting missiles all over the place. The mind doesn't know that the body isn't doing it yet."

Okay, I could do that—visualizing myself hitting a gapper for a double.

"Are you trying to hit everything up there? What are you doing? Looking for a fast ball and adjusting to off-speed with every pitch?"

Tommy had me there. I was one of those "sit fastball" hitters looking for a fastball with every pitch. Funny how I'd never get a fastball with the game on the line, which meant I was looking for something I wasn't going to get.

Tommy explained how much I could learn from watching the game, even when I wasn't hitting. "Keep an eye on that pitcher," he said. "That'll give you a better feel of what he'll throw you in certain counts."

Tommy stood up and started pacing his hotel room. "I want you looking for what you're going to get pitched, not what you want to hit," he said. "We all want to hit a fastball, but sometimes it's okay to sit on an off-speed if you think you're going to get it. I want you hunting speeds—sitting fastball or sitting off-speed until you get two strikes. It's way easier hitting one pitch when you know it's coming than three when you don't."

I'd never heard a coach break down hitting like Tommy did. Everything he said made sense to me. He got me watching the game in a new way. I began applying his principles and started hunting speeds and stopped trying to hit everything thrown my way.

I felt Tommy put me on the right track. This is where the mental game kicked in for me and why some of my most productive years happened in the last third of my 14-year baseball career.

I must have listened to that tape of Tommy McCraw every day of the baseball season for the next seven years. If I was in my car, that audiocassette tape was playing. Teri would say, "Really? Do we have to listen to this crap again?"

"Yes, honey," I would patiently reply. "Hearing this tape makes me a better hitter."

I stopped listening after I retired. Unfortunately, I lost Tommy's tape in one of our moves. I'll always believe that if I had known at age twenty-one or twenty-two what I learned from Tommy in my late twenties, my baseball career would have been a much different story.

So years later, when I was a baseball agent, I had a brainstorm: my players needed help with their mental game, and if I could help them perform well at the plate, then they would become better hitters, which would make me more money as an agent.

I decided to go into a recording studio and deliver a monologue on what constituted a "quality at-bat." I wrote down some notes and then sat behind a microphone and shared many of the principles that Tommy impressed upon me for forty-five minutes. I also added my thoughts on the best mental approach that hitters could take to the plate each time they had an at-bat.

I called my CD *The Mental Side* and pressed 500 copies. I gave those CDs to anyone who would take them, especially college baseball coaches in the Los Angeles area.

George Horton, the Cal State Fullerton manager and architect of one of the most successful college baseball teams in the last twenty-five years, liked my CD so much that he had his entire team listen to *The Mental Side* five hours before the start of a three-game series against the No. 1-ranked team in the country, the University of Miami.

Cal State Fullerton swept the Hurricanes baseball team—in Florida—scoring in the double digits each game. "Your CD changed the way my guys played," he said.

That's when I knew I had something. I started speaking before any baseball team or group who'd take me. I spoke at baseball camps sponsored by the University of Southern California, UC Irvine, and Cal State Fullerton. All this led to requests to speak before dozens of other college teams around the country as well as high school teams and travel ball teams.

I called my budding speaking business Quality at-Bats and have been on the road for the better part of fifteen years. I also got into coaching in 2008 when the Toronto Blue Jays asked me to work with their minor league players on the mental side of hitting. They called me a "performance coach."

This is why, in Part II of *Spring Time*, I want to talk about the most important part of hitting—the mental side. If you're a young player or the parent of a budding baseball player or softball player, I urge you to read the next chapter.

LAST PITCH

*I*n fourteen seasons of professional baseball, I spent only thirty-six days in the major leagues.

That short stretch is called a "cup of coffee," meaning that the player was only in the big leagues long enough to have a cup of coffee before being returned to the minors. There are several "cup of coffee" players who became famous for their short stays in the majors, the most notable being Moonlight Graham, who played two innings in the outfield for the 1905 New York Giants and left baseball to become a doctor in Chisholm, Minnesota. His story is the emotional center point for the movie *Field of Dreams*, starring Kevin Costner.

I have a different story—but one I believe is worthy of the

silver screen as well. For most of my youth, people told me that I was too small to play baseball. I was that tiny kid who sat at the end of the bench, wondering if I would ever get big enough to play against kids my age. I was the shortest boy in my class who wore a way-too-big uniform as he trudged to the first base coaching box and waved his arms for my teammate to keep running to second after hitting a line-drive shot to the alley. I was the little brother who was told that the only reason I was on the team was because my older brother Gary was a star.

Plenty of people told me I would never make it. Many more never said that to my face, but I could tell by their dismissive looks or their collective shrugs that they never thought I'd amount to anything—on or off the baseball field.

And yet I did make it—all the way to the major leagues, no less. I truly feel I am the baseball version of *Rudy*, and even better, I ended up playing in the BIG LEAGUES, as brief as it was—eight games with 17 at-bats and two hits in each league.

The odds of getting there were and still are incredibly daunting. According to the NCAA, of the 450,000 high school baseball players in this country, only the top 5 percent will wind up playing on a college team. Once you're playing college baseball, the odds of getting drafted by a major league team are one in ten, and from the minor leagues, only 10 percent of minor leaguers ever make to The Show. In other words, of the 450,000 high school athletes who play baseball each year, only 225 or .0005 percent—that's one out of 2,000—will ever step onto a major league field.

Consider how this stat relates to me. During my senior year of high school, I sat on the bench and coached first base. Yet out of 2,000 high school ballplayers in Orange County at that time, I was the one who made the big leagues against tremendous odds.

I wouldn't blame anyone for thinking that I would have been

the last person to put on a Major League baseball uniform. Heck, no one thought I was going to play baseball in college, let alone the minor leagues or a Major League team like the Cleveland Indians or New York Mets.

But that's not the reason I've written *Spring Time*. I've gone to the effort to share my story because I want to inspire you—the young ballplayer as well as your parents—to never give up. While the odds are highly unlikely that you'll ever reach the major leagues, don't let anyone tell you that you're too small to play baseball or that you cannot get a college education out of this game. There are so many colleges and universities around the country that are looking for good baseball and softball players, and they have scholarships to offer.

Baseball is the greatest game in the world, and you don't have to be tall to play it. Take a look at Dustin Pedroia, the Boston Red Sox second baseman who's 5 feet, 7 inches with a good pair of cleats on. He could shrink another two inches and still be a Major League All-Star because he's one of the best competitors in the world. That's what it takes to get to the big leagues and stay there.

I close with this thought:

I've been in professional baseball for thirty-five years. I thank God for everything that's happened to me. I thank all my teammates and coaches who helped me grow as a player and a person. I wouldn't change a whole lot except for one thing: I wish I had given school my best effort. If there was one mistake I made, I wish I had listened to my dad and applied myself to my studies. That I regret.

So young readers, learn from me, listen to your parents, and work hard to get good grades.

And then go out and make your own Spring Time.

My parents, Gene and Sharon Springer, met at a roller-skating rink in Santa Ana, California, when Dad was in the Marines and stationed at Camp Pendleton. For the first six months of their relationship, he told my mom that his name was "Dick Fox"—just in case. When they fell in love, Dad came clean, and they eloped in Las Vegas. Kids came quickly: Gary, followed by me (bottom photo, center), followed by Susan. A fourth child, Robin, arrived a year later, so my parents had four children in four years. I got my athletic talent from my mother (pictured in stripes), who was a top amateur bowler and excellent softball player. My father wasn't a natural athlete.

We grew up in the Sixties in Huntington Beach, California, a time when the "car culture" reigned in Southern California. My mom loved having our portraits taken, but notice that I was the only child not looking at the camera when Gary, Susan, and Robin posed for this photo.

WESTMINSTER
NATIONAL LITTLE LEAGUE
1969

Dad worked a lot for a company that built sheet metal buildings, but he always made sure he was involved in our youth sports. In this team picture, taken when I was eight years old, my father is the adult on the left, and I'm in the front row, first from the left. The following year, at the age of nine, I was promoted to the Major Division and played on a Little League team with my brother, Gary. Dad was our coach. Believe it or not, we got all four kids and all our luggage into our Dodge station wagon for the long drive in Minnesota to see Dad's family.

W E S T M I N S T E R   S C H O O L   D I S T R I C T   **STEVE SPRINGER**
CONFERENCE WORK SHEET
Grades 4-6

READING Below ☐ Gr.Level At ☑ Gr.Level Above ☐ Gr.Level

Comments or Suggestions

Very poor reading habits. Has done very poor on understanding because he won't take time.

Reads various materials ___
Dictionary skills ___
Basic skills ___   (Vowels ___ Alphabet ___)
Vocabulary ✓
Comprehension ✓

MATH Below Gr.Level ___ At Gr.Level ✓ Above Gr.Level ___

Reads numerals ___
Knows place value ___
Multiplication facts ___
Addition facts ___
Subtraction facts ___   Regrouping ___
Basic facts ___
Geometry ___   Graphs ___

Steve is extremely careless in math. He doesn't completely listen to instructions so it takes him longer to understand new concepts. Needs to work on accuracy instead of speed.

SOCIAL STUDIES

Maps skill ___
Special reports ___   *Science*
Reference materials ___
Historic comprehension ✓

Steve needs to slow down when taking a test — also when doing regular assignments.

HANDWRITING

Letter formation
Neatness   *Sloppy*

Spelling is not natural subject for Steve + he needs to work at it a little more.

SPELLING

Assigned words ___
Everyday use ___

STUDY HABITS   **CITIZENSHIP**

Completes assignments ___
Obeys school rules ___

Language average in a C. He could do better.

Read it and weep: this is the work sheet my parents received at a parent-teacher conference when I was attended Ada Clegg Elementary School in Huntington Beach. I wish I put as much effort into my schoolwork as I did into playing baseball. As you can see, I was a poor student, and that ended up costing me a baseball scholarship to UCLA.

I was the smallest kid in my class growing up, and by the time I entered high school, I was only 4 feet, 11 inches tall. Naturally, I was at a disadvantage on the baseball field. I got only three at-bats my freshman year, saw more action my sophomore and junior years on the JV team, but sat on the varsity bench for most of my senior year even though I had grown to 5 feet, 6 inches. When I graduated from high school, no college wanted me to play, so I enrolled at a local junior college, Golden West College, and hoped to make the team there.

STEVE TURNING A double play against Wilson Bakersfield

We only lived twenty miles from Disneyland, where my uncle, Gary Wakefield, oversaw operations at Frontierland. Consequently, we could go to the Magic Kingdom any time we wanted—which was a lot since we got free passes. Mom was so into Disneyland that she insisted that we wait on the sidewalk for the afternoon parade at least an hour before the floats came by. Following high school graduation, Uncle Gary helped me get a job on the Davy Crockett Canoes attraction, which really built up the strength in my arms.

Disneyland.
PICTURE
PASSPORT

Disneyland

SUPPORT YOUR LOCAL CANOERS

Several weeks of hard training and lack of sleep will culminate tomorrow when 12 canoe teams battle it out for a winning time in the 18th Annual Canoe Race finals. Come out and cheer your favorite team to victory from 6:00 to 8:30 a.m. Refreshments will be available at the Hungry Bear Restaurant.

STEVE'S TEAM   (Photo by James Russell)
CAME IN SECOND

Below are the top teams that qualified for semifinal rounds earlier this week. Check the Cast Activities bulletin board for tomorrow's finalists.

Family has always been important to us. A fifth child, Cori (above, on the left), arrived when I was in high school. I'm in the back with Susan and Robin, while Gary is seated next to Grandma Kiefer, our great-grandmother from Seal Beach, California.

After a standout season at the University of Utah my junior year, I was drafted by the New York Mets in the 20th round, which was a miracle in itself. I rose steadily in the minor leagues: rookie ball to Single-A to Double-A to Triple-A in four years. By this time, I had my "man body," meaning I was six feet tall and 170 pounds.

Who's that ripped ballplayer spraying the champagne? That's me giving my Tidewater Tides teammates a fizzy shower after we won the International League championship in 1987. The other shot is from a close play at first base, where Willie Aikens, who played eight years in the majors, tried to pick me off.

You don't have to be a Major League player to be on a baseball card. Here's a sampling of my baseball cards during my fourteen seasons in the minor leagues.

ProCards

STEVE SPRINGER
Infield
Colorado Springs

TIDEWATER TIDES

STEVE SPRINGER   IF

TIDEWATER TIDES

STEVE SPRINGER   IF

STEVE SPRINGER

PRE-ROOKIE '91

Infield

STEVE SPRINGER

Sky Box   Pre-Rookie '92

Tidewater Tides   Infield

PRO CARDS

STEVE
SPRINGER
NORFOLK TIDES • IF

When I finally made it to the Major Leagues in 1990, Mom slapped newspaper clippings on a piece of plywood to mark the event. She was my biggest fan. I was one happy dude to receive the call-up to the Cleveland Indians, but my trip to the big leagues was short-lived.

I met my wife, Teri, in Newport Beach, California. We got married just before the 1990 season, and my mother wished me all the best.

Our first child, Cody, who arrived in 1991, stands with me when I played a season with the Toledo Mud Hens. Teri is pictured shortly after giving birth to our daughter Logan.

Call this my "Tribute to Mom" page . . . Sharon Springer was a lovely woman, the type who was always volunteering to help out and bring treats to ballgames. She's pictured here with a close friend, Jan McGlothlin, whose husband, Jim, pitched for the California Angels. Jim tragically died of leukemia at the age of thirty-two.

Teri and I are blessed with two great kids—Cody and Logan. Both in their mid-twenties, Cody is a budding entrepreneur and Logan is working as a nanny and dabbling in school.

From 2008 through the 2016 season, I was the "performance coach" for the Toronto Blue Jays, working with their minor league players on the mental side of hitting. I also consult with a number of Major League players including these three All-Stars (bottom photo, from the left): Nolan Arenado, who led the National League in home runs and RBIs in 2015 and 2016; A.J. Pollock, who batted .315 in 2015; Paul Goldschmidt, a tough-hitting first baseman who has a career .299 average. I'm also pictured with Mark Trumbo, an American League All-Star who lead the majors in home runs in 2016. I strongly believe my calling in life is to stand up before young ballplayers, with bat in hand, and talk to them about the all-important mental side of hitting.

PART II

Hitting a Baseball

15

Batter Up . . .

I love speaking to youngsters and their parents about hitting, which Ted Williams, arguably the greatest hitter of all time, once described as the "hardest single thing to do in sports."

The act of hitting a baseball has a lot to do with hand-eye coordination and timing. It's all about your ability to synchronize the swing of the bat with the exact time and location of the pitch's arrival at home plate—in approximately .395 seconds. If your timing is off by a tenth of a second, you'll swing and hit nothing but air. But if your timing is perfect, you'll hit the ball hard or a long way.

What I've just described is the physical side of hitting a baseball, which involves incredible hand-eye coordination. To help you with the mechanics of hitting, I'd have to meet with you for a hitting lesson and watch your swing. Since that's not possible in a book, let me pivot and focus on the mental side of hitting and the importance of feeling confident each time you step into the batter's box. I know from personal experience that a confident Steve Springer was a good hitter but an unsure and insecure Steve Springer sucked at the plate.

That's why I devote so much time to talking about the mental aspect of hitting. When Yogi Berra famously quipped, "Baseball is 90 percent mental and the other half is physical," we can all share a laugh, even though I probably matched Yogi's math skills when I was in middle school. Which leads me to this question: If baseball is 90 percent mental, why do we work on the mental side so little—surely less than 10 percent of the time? If every player spent as much time mentally preparing for an at-bat as he did practicing his swing, he would become a much better hitter.

The gold standard in baseball is being a .300 hitter, which means three hits in ten at-bats. We are all aware of the vast difference between a .300 hitter versus a .200 hitter. The former will play in the major leagues and earn many millions of dollars, while the latter will be out of baseball before too long—all because of the difference in one at-bat out of ten! I believe the best way to become a .300 hitter is to change your definition of success to this: *When I hit the ball hard, I help my team win.*

You see, when you hit the ball hard, you will have a *much* better chance of getting a hit against a defense that outnumbers you nine-to-one. Hitting the ball hard in fair territory has a way of resulting in more hits, and every base hit raises your batting average. But in order to get three hits in every ten at-bats, I believe you need to have at least six or seven quality at-bats in those ten at-bats. That's where your focus needs to be.

Now that I've gotten this off my chest, this is the last time I'm going to talk about the batting average, which is the biggest trap in baseball. In fact, when I speak before baseball groups, I call the batting average "Satan" and declare that the batting average is evil. I've seen how worrying about the batting average can destroy young kids at every level of baseball and softball because hitting is hitting. It's horrible how kids are tormented by their batting average, which is hung around their necks like an anchor.

Sure, coaches and scouts are fixated on the batting average. I get that. I know the first thing your friends or your parents ask is "How many hits did you get today?" or "What's your batting average now?" But I want you to put the batting average aside. If possible, I'm asking you to rid it from your mind because the batting average isn't the best indicator for your ability to hit a baseball.

You know why? Because I bet you've had games where you hit three balls right on the screws but right at someone, meaning each swing resulted in an out. When that happens, think about the positive: you beat the pitcher. The pitcher knows you beat him. Heck, even the pitcher's *mom* knows you beat him. Yet baseball says you suck because your batting average went down. It makes no sense.

I've never asked the players I've worked with to get three hits in a game, and I'm not going to do that to you now. You have my permission *not* to get three hits, which is something I wish I had given myself when I was playing. Sure, baseball can be a frustrating game filled with uncontrollable factors, but you can give yourself permission to fail.

There's no reason to fret about past at-bats. Instead, sweep those negative thoughts out of your mind and concentrate on being the best competitor you can be on the field. That starts with keeping this attainable goal in mind: *Hit the ball hard.* Believe me: good hitters line out more. Get good at lining out.

When you take this approach to hitting a baseball, you'll be stepping up to the plate with the mindset of having a "quality" at-bat.

What constitutes a quality trip to the plate? Anything that falls into one of these eight categories:

1. Any base hit
2. Any hard-hit ball

3. Any time you move a teammate to the next base
4. Any RBI
5. A successful bunt
6. A base on balls
7. Being hit by a pitch
8. Making the pitcher work by fouling off pitches and lasting at least eight pitches in an at-bat.

By keeping your focus on hitting the ball hard or doing any of the other things I've listed above, your self-confidence and self-esteem aren't tied up into getting a base hit but rather this: Did you have a quality at-bat and help the team? In the long run, you're going to become a better hitter and more valuable to your teammates if you're thinking about getting a quality at-bat instead of a hit. Think in this manner: *Every day I have a new game, a new pitcher, and a chance to be a new hero. I'm not going to let my batting average or yesterday's 0-for-4 dictate how I feel today.*

I know that there will be times when you'll hit a blooper to the outfield and get credited with a hit, but they should be viewed as something akin to finding a $20 bill on the sidewalk: unexpected but not counted upon. But old habits die hard. I remember what Clint Hurdle, my manager at the Tidewater Tides and the skipper of Pittsburgh Pirates since 2011, once told me: "It's amazing that players would rather hit a ball off the knuckles that drops in-between two diving fielders than hit a line-drive rocket at somebody."

When I was playing for Clint, he used to mark a "Q" next to the players' names on the lineup card whenever they logged a quality at-bat. He also did his research and discovered that if a team had at least 15 productive team plate appearances in a game, they would win more than 60 percent of their games.

After I became the performance coach for the Toronto Blue Jays,

I convinced the front office to put some reward money out there for every quality at-bat. For each of the Blue Jay's minor league teams, the managers started handing out $25 gift cards to Best Buy to the three players who logged the most quality at-bats in the last week. It was amazing what a little extra spending money did to change attitudes on the bench. The program was a resounding success and lifted the confidence of all their players, especially those in the midst of a 2-for-25 funk.

I wonder what would happen if every major league team invested $500,000 in a reward program with their minor league affiliates. They could offer $100 to every player for every quality at-bat but only on nights the team won. I'm convinced that would work, and here's why.

Let's say that every position player averaged two quality at-bats in each victory. If a minor league team won 80 games in a 142-game season, that's $1,600 in rewards each night. Over the course of the season, that would cost the major league front office $128,000 in bonuses per each team in their farm system. That's chump change for major league organizations with budgets in the hundreds of millions of dollars. I know it's a pipe dream, but I still think it's a good idea.

Whether it's rewards or through hearing my message, baseball needs to jump on the bandwagon of quality at-bats.

THE QAB

*H*ere's another idea that I'd like to see happen in baseball: adding the quality at-bat to a player's batting statistics. Let's call it the QAB—for quality at-bat—and have that number listed right after the batting average.

What a great measuring tool the QAB would be! In addition to statistics like on-base percentage and slugging average, the QAB would show players, coaches, and the front office how valuable players are to the team from an offensive perspective.

In fact, I think the QAB would be an even better measuring stick than the OBP—or on-base percentage, which measures how often a batter reaches base. The OBP's complete formula is the number of hits, base on balls, and hit-by-pitches divided by the number of at-bats, walks, hit-by-pitches, and sacrifices flies. Mike Trout of the Los Angeles Angels led the majors in the OBP with a .441 average in 2016.

The formula for the QAB would begin by adding up the number of quality at-bats—as defined by one of the eight categories I listed on pages 167-168—and dividing that number by the total number of at-bats. I'm thinking that someone like Mike Trout—who I can tell marches up to the plate with the mindset of hitting the ball hard somewhere—would have a QAB in the .600 range, maybe more.

Sure, what constitutes a "hard-hit ball" is subjective, but the official scorer makes judgment calls all game long on whether batted balls are hits or errors. By taking the focus off the batting average and putting it directly on the number of quality at-bats, baseball becomes a better game because the hitting gets better.

Of course, pitchers would hate the QAB. They wouldn't want to see players walking up to the plate with confidence and an attainable goal to hit the ball hard. Trust me, their ERAs would skyrocket. For all these reasons, I'd like someone into sabermetrics—an empirical analysis of baseball—to champion the QAB, which would be a great way to find undervalued players.

A radical idea like the QAB has to be done because teams are hitting less and scoring fewer runs than they have in a generation, while strikeouts have hit historic levels in recent years. Strikeouts as a percentage of total plate appearances reached 21.1 percent in 2016, way up from 2004, when the strikeout percentage was 16.5 percent. In 2016, hitters struck out 38,982 times, the ninth straight year in which an all-time record was set.

Yes, I know that pitching is incredible today, but I submit that players are striking out more often because they are swinging for the fences since home-run hitters will always have a place in the batting lineup and get paid the big bucks. Home runs increased by 17 percent in 2015 and another 14 percent in 2016 to 5,610 circuit clouts, just 83 home runs short of the all-time record set in 2000 when the Steroid Era of baseball was in full bloom.

Just because more fly balls are leaving the ballpark doesn't mean you should be swinging for the fences. Unless you're hitting 30-plus bombs a year, chasing the home run ball is a fool's errand.

Here's another trend I see: too many batters are swinging defensively instead of trying to drive the ball when they have count leverage at 1-0, 2-0, and 3-1. When you have the mindset of having a quality at-bat, you'll be swinging *offensively* with those counts. You'll discover freedom for your abilities to come out. You'll swing with confidence instead of worrying about whether you're going to get a base hit. When you hit the ball hard, you beat the pitcher. If you get a hit, that's a bonus. Trust me, your team will win many more games than it will lose when you and your teammates are looking to have a quality at-bat.

I know my message is resonating. When I spoke to the woman's softball teams at the University of Oregon and Notre Dame about the batting average being a trap, the players got it. They responded by putting their focus on making quality at-bats, which helped their teams experience great success. I even heard that the Oregon and Notre Dame players stopped talking about their batting average. That's the attitude you want.

Mickey Mantle, the all-time Yankee great from the 1950s and '60s, was one of those players who had the right attitude. The story goes that one time he was in the locker room before an All-Star game, talking about hitting with another player who wanted to know if Mickey held his elbow in, led with his hip or his knee, how he leveled his shoulders, and other details of swinging his bat.

Mickey had no idea what the other player was driving at. "I don't think about anything," the Mick said. "I just try to hit the ball as hard as I can."

BUILDING SELF-ESTEEM

I've always said that baseball is the biggest self-esteem–destroying game there is, especially for Little Leaguers. Baseball has a way of making kids feel worthless and like nobodies.

Parents, I know you love your children. I understand that you view them as your little Messiahs. I did, too, when my son, Cody, and daughter, Logan, were growing up. But even the best kids in the world are susceptible to getting mentally steamrolled when playing competitive baseball or girls softball.

Let's say your Little Johnny makes an error to lose a game. The other team is cheering the unexpected victory. His coaches are yelling at him or showing their disgust, and his teammates hang their heads on the way to the dugout. Some even throw their gloves. So for one error, Little Johnny is getting beat up by his coaches and teammates as well as his parents, family members, and friends watching the game.

If you're not careful, he's going to quit playing baseball—maybe not now but surely by the time he's thirteen years old. I'm telling you, baseball loses more kids at the age of thirteen than any other sport. Part of that has to do with the graduation from a Little League–sized ball field to a regulation–sized diamond, but the main reason is because of the pressure put on kids by the people who love them the most—us parents. Not to mention how baseball never builds a kid's self-esteem.

The same advice goes for parents of softball players. We all have to be careful what we say and how we react when our kids let a ground ball roll through their legs or they strike out with the game on the line.

I recently ran into a dad who knew I was a baseball guy. When I asked him what he was up to, he told me he was coaching his seven-year-old's travel ball team. Yes, in Southern California they have travel teams for second-graders.

"Nice," I replied. "So you know you're coaching the biggest self-esteem-destroying sport in the world?"

"What?"

"Yeah. When your son makes an error, he wants to cry. The other team is cheering like crazy, and he doesn't like that. The coach is yelling at him—and that's you. He doesn't like that. Then he has to ride home with you and sit across from you at the dinner table. So for one error, your son is going to get beat up four times. If you're not careful, he's going to quit playing baseball by the time he's thirteen."

Two months later, I was at a sports bar enjoying a pizza and watching Mark Trumbo—whom I've worked with for a long time—play for the Angels. The same guy walked up to me.

"You changed my life," he said.

"What are you talking about?"

"When you told me my son was playing the biggest self-esteem-destroying sport in the world, you hit me square in the teeth. I was so embarrassed that I couldn't even talk. Now I'm the most positive coach on the field. I watch what I say to my players, especially after an error or a strikeout. When I hear another coach yell at seven-year-old ballplayers, I cringe. I decided that I'm going to make baseball fun for my son, which is why I take him out for an ice cream after every game. And my ex-wife wants to remarry me because she can't believe it's me."

True story.

Mom and Dad, I don't want you to put so much pressure on your sons and daughters not to make mistakes because it's inevitable they'll mess up. Failure is part of the game. Never forget that they're still in their little kid bodies and are emotionally immature.

That's why the twelve-and-under years—12U—are the toughest ages to play baseball and softball. When I coached Cody's team with Rich Ameral, a former major leaguer for ten seasons, we put white Q stickers on the back of their helmets if they had a quality at-bat. After a while, that's all our players wanted—a sticker on their helmet after a hard-hit ground out, a sacrifice fly, or a successful bunt, so we changed what their definition of success was.

We had one player who, to be charitable, lacked any coordination. When he *fouled off* a ball, we made him feel like he was Mike Trout by giving him a white sticker on his helmet. For this young player, that was his definition of success.

Let me tell you, he was so happy to get those stickers. His parents were thrilled because nobody had ever built their son up in sports, but we did, and that made us feel good.

Here's the big picture of why it's important to build up a player's self-esteem: It's likely that only three or four ballplayers from a Little League team will be good enough to play high school baseball. From that group, only a couple of high school players, at the most, can play college baseball. And from a college team, if one kid goes on to play pro baseball, that's unbelievable. Yet every one of those boys on a youth baseball team will grow up to be men—and the girl softball players will grow up to be women. I want their ball-playing experiences to be positive because they are participating in a sport that can teach the greatest lessons about life: how to fail, how to be a good teammate, how to lose, and how to win.

Rich and I also gave stickers to every player who got hit by a pitch, which is huge at that age. Why? Because it's during Little League baseball that kids find out if they're tough enough to play this game after getting hit by a pitch for the first time. There's a Joel Willett in every league.

Whenever I speak before baseball groups, I'll say this: "Kids, the fear of getting hit by a pitch is real. The possibility of getting plunked puts great fear into every batter. But I'll tell you what: the next time you get hit by a pitch, your parents are going to give you $10 if you don't cry."

You should see the surprised looks from the moms and dads in the audience, but a reward system works. I wish I had received some ice cream money after flame-throwing Joel Willett nailed me when I was nine years old. I might not have developed some bad hitting habits, like bailing out whenever a pitch was high and tight.

Hitting is tough enough without worrying about how much it's going to hurt from getting struck with a pitched baseball. Standing in the batter's box—all exposed to getting walloped by a pitch—can be extremely hard to mentally cope with.

We've all had days where we've done everything right at the plate and gone home with the sour taste of an 0-for-4 in our mouths. The ability to handle failure is paramount in baseball. This is why we need to change the definition of success. I want you to forget the past quickly, maintain a short memory, focus on making your next at-bat a quality at-bat, and stop worrying about your batting average.

THAT EXTRA AT-BAT

When you're 0-for-3, you have to want that fourth at-bat late in a game.

I know how easy it is to have a horrible day at the plate, whiffing twice and hitting a pop-up caught in foul territory. Many 0-for-3 hitters mentally bag it if they come up for a fourth time in a game, muttering to themselves, "This isn't my day."

You're letting your mind get in the way of your ability. There will be up-and-down periods over the course of the season—or slumps. I don't like to use that word because slumps are for players chasing their batting average, which I've described as evil.

But think about this: If you were fortunate enough to have ten quality at-bats out of ten plate appearances, don't you think it's possible that you might get *one more* hit in those ten at-bats? And if you got an extra hit in every ten at-bats, what would that do to your batting average? (I know . . . the batting average is evil. I'm just seeing if you're paying attention.)

One of the players I've advised and developed a close relationship with is Mark Trumbo, who grew up in nearby Anaheim and is one of the premier home-run hitters in baseball at the age of thirty. Mark, who plays first base for the Baltimore Orioles, led the major leagues in home runs with 47 during the 2016 season.

Mark embraces the idea of "wanting" his fourth or even fifth at-bat when he's having an "0-fer" night. "If you start hearing those voices saying, 'You've got to get a hit right here,' the pressure goes right through the roof," he said. "If you keep it simple and say your goal is to hit the ball hard, you can deal with whatever happens. This makes batting much easier."

One time, Mark was 0-for-4 with two strikeouts late in a home game against the Detroit Tigers. Then, in extra innings, Mark took it deep for a walk-off home run, and the game was over.

"I can't tell you how many times I've gone through a whole game 0-for-3 or 0-for-4 with some absolutely terrible at-bats," Mark said. "But I've learned from Spring that every at-bat counts, and the last at-bat is when *heroes* are made. Now I have the mindset that there's damage to be done and I can be the hero late in the game, which keeps me mentally where I need to be."

I know that maintaining a positive mental approach is easier said than done, especially after several hitless trips to the plate. But the key element to hitting is *psychological*. (I joke with audiences that I couldn't spell *psychological* out loud if my baseball career depended upon it, but I do know that the long word starts with an "s.")

But at the end of the day, hitting is about the mind. That's why first-round draft picks can't get out of Single-A ball and why guys who don't get drafted spend ten years in the big leagues. It's about having the mind and the heart to compete with confidence.

As part of my duties with the Blue Jays, I prepared audio files for each of the players in which I shared tips and reminders tailored to each team member. Many of my mini-talks, which the players listened to on their smartphones, were designed to help them stay confident and become the best hitters possible.

In addition, I also act as a hitting mentor to several dozen major league baseball hitters on a regular basis. A few of the notables are:

- PAUL GOLDSCHMIDT, the first baseman for the Arizona Diamondbacks who has a career .299 batting average and been a National League All-Star four times. Paul said, "Steve Springer has helped me take my mental game to the next level, and he can do that for you, too."

- **A.J. Pollock**, a Diamondback teammate who batted .315 in 2015 but missed the 2016 season after breaking his right elbow sliding into home plate in a spring training game. The Notre Dame graduate said, "I got Spring's CD when I was a sophomore in college, and I wish I had it when I was a sophomore in high school."

- **Nolan Arenado**, an exceptionally skilled third baseman with the Colorado Rockies. Nolan has already been an All-Star twice in his four seasons of big league baseball and led the National League in home runs and RBIs in 2015 and 2016. The sky is the limit for Noland. "When I get into a funk, Spring knows he's getting a phone call," he said.

- **Mark Trumbo**, who I just talked about, is a two-time All-Star and was the major league leader in home runs in 2016. He's also hit 178 home runs in seven seasons. I've worked with Mark for ten years, and he has one of the best attitudes in baseball. He *always* wants that next at-bat.

- **Randal Grichuk**, a centerfielder for the St. Louis Cardinals, is known for his raw power and bat speed. During the season, he calls me once a week for a mental tune-up and calls me his "Hitting Whisperer."

Finally, there's one more player I want to mention, but first I have to share a little story. Around seven or eight years ago, I was at an off-season conference for baseball players and their wives in Phoenix, Arizona. We had a breakout session, where I joined a small group of seven guys. We went around the horn and introduced ourselves.

"Hi," I began. "I'm Steve Springer, the performance coach with the Blue Jays."

I noticed that one of the guys, who looked to be around twenty years old, broke out in a wide smile. I'd seen that look a million times.

"You got my CD, don't you, buddy," I said.

The young ballplayers cracked up. "Spring, I can't believe you're here. I've had your CD for five years."

He said his name was Jonathan Gilmore, and he was a minor leaguer. He had been drafted in the first round by the Atlanta Braves in the 2007 MLB June Amateur Draft, the thirty-third player taken.

"I can't wait until I tell my brother-in-law that you're here," he said. "He's going to flip out."

"Who's your brother-in-law?"

"Ben Zobrist. He's listened to your CD as well."

"Really?"

"Yeah."

I met Ben for the first time later that night. He said he got my CD in 2006 when he was twenty-five years old and in Double-A. Midway through that season, he got his first call-up to the major leagues with the Tampa Bay Rays—and what a career he's put together since then. Within three years, he was named to the American League All-Star team. Now he's on top of the baseball world after being named the 2016 World Series MVP when his team, the Chicago Cubs, won the World Series for the first time since 1908. (Ben also received a World Series ring the year before while playing for the Kansas City Royals.)

Ben wrapped me in a bear hug after we met for the first time. "Dude, your CD changed the way I thought about hitting," he said. "I used to think batting average, batting average all the time. I wasn't confident at the plate when I wasn't getting hits, but after listening to you, I told myself that I don't care what my average is."

I love hearing stories like that—and watching success stories like Ben Zobrist happen. He didn't get better physically. He got better mentally.

But here's something else to keep in mind: Ben and all these great guys have been excellent hitters since they were eight years old. They grew up with superior hitting mechanics, which I define as:

- slow feet
- fast hands
- quiet head
- trying to hit the inside part of the ball

All these elements can be worked on in batting practice. These superior hitters are what I call "pitch hunters," which means they go up to the plate with a confidence and a plan, based on their study of the pitcher on the mound. They trust their ability and have forgotten what happened the previous week, the previous day, or even the previous at-bat. They practice staying calm and being mentally tough.

If you embrace the idea of stepping up to the plate and hitting the ball hard somewhere, and getting your teammates to do the same, the freedom to compete with confidence will be infectious in the dugout. Believe me, your team will have a better chance of winning.

Here's another point about the batting average—it's what happened yesterday and the day before that and the day before that. The pitcher today doesn't give a hoot about yesterday, and neither should you. Believe it or not, I'm really trying to help you hit your highest batting average, so let's get the right player to stand in the batting box every single at bat every single game. What I do need from you is for you to strive to be the best competitor on the field with the attainable goal of hitting the ball hard and helping your team win. Let me tell you, I have this exact conversation with every major league baseball player who calls me for a tune-up during the season.

One thing I also tell all my players is to make every single game like it's Opening Day. There's nothing like the first game of the baseball season. It's a time when every player starts at the same place, a time of new beginning where hope and optimism reigns. You want to feel the same tingly feeling of excitement that you do when a new season starts for every at-bat.

Nobody who ever played baseball for a living suited up on Opening Day with zero confidence. Why is that? Because they didn't have yesterday getting in their way today.

If you can have the same positive attitude each time you step in the batter's box, I'm confident that you'll be blown away by how much success you will have with each quality at-bat.

16

Extra Innings

*W*henever I speak or conduct a hitting clinic, I share my story of how I grew up as the smallest kid in my class and was constantly told that I could never become a baseball player. I also describe my feelings of being left out and the insecurity I felt sitting at the end of the bench and coaching first base for most of my high school years as well as my freshman season at Golden West College.

And then I recount how I was finally able to play well in my sophomore year of junior college and how that strong season propelled me to the University of Utah. And then I had a breakout 5-for-5 day with fifty major league baseball scouts in the grandstands, which led me to being drafted by the New York Mets in the 20th round. After signing a pro contract, I spent eight long, long years in the minor leagues until I was finally called up by the Cleveland Indians.

My story is filled with ups and downs, which mirrors life, I suppose. I know that without my unique life experiences, I wouldn't be in the position I'm in today, which is being a mentor to the next generation of baseball hitters.

I love standing before audiences and talking about how the batting average is a trap. I enjoy teaching about how to watch the pitcher and hunt pitches because too many hitters are ready to hit everything but not ready for anything. I take pleasure in detailing how to hit the ball properly and attacking the inside part of the baseball. I appreciate how I can point out the importance of breathing, slowing the game down, and being a good teammate. I'm grateful that I can stress the importance of defense, lifting weights, and making the long toss from one side of the outfield to the other. I love bringing up stories of big leaguers who've bought into what I teach. And I look forward to closing my talks by telling everyone that God is real and loves everyone of us.

I want to finish *Spring Time* talking about the role of God in my life. Let me begin by saying that for many years, I had God sitting behind a billboard with a radar gun, waiting to trap me. That's not who He is. He is love and grace and mercy and even more grace. That's what I've learned from Pete McKenzie. He's a former minor league player who leads the Influencers West men's ministry (influencerswest.org) that I attend weekly in Orange County.

If hearing this message doesn't interest you, there's no reason to read on. I appreciate that you've stuck with me this far, and I sincerely wish you all the best as you pursue your goals in baseball or softball.

But if you want to read further, I hope you'll open up your heart and hear what I have to say. I'm confident that you'll be touched by the "rest of the story."

MEETING MICKEY

*W*hen Joe Redfield and I flew to Utica, New York, to start our professional baseball careers in June 1982, we stopped in Atlanta, where we changed planes and met another rookie minor leaguer who'd be joining us in Little Falls.

His name was Mickey Weston. Born a month after me, Mickey had grown up in Flint, Michigan, and been a star pitcher at Eastern Michigan University.

I like to tell friends that Mickey was the second guy I met in pro baseball. When Joe and I introduced ourselves in Atlanta, I immediately sensed there was something different about Mickey—and it wasn't because he was dressed in a three-piece suit for the airline flight while Joe and I were California casual in T-shirts and blue jeans.

You know how you click with certain people right away? That's how things were with Mickey, who was friendly, encouraging, and ambitious. He also made it known he was a Christian. He seemed to be as comfortable in his faith as I was in my baseball uniform.

We weren't in Little Falls more than a couple of weeks when he dropped by my locker before a game. "Spring, we're having Baseball Chapel before the game on Sunday. Can you come?"

"What's Baseball Chapel?" I asked. This was something new to me, but I'd only been a professional ballplayer for two weeks.

"In pro baseball, from the major leagues all the way down to where we are in rookie ball, every team has a Baseball Chapel representative drop by on Sunday before the game," Mickey explained. "It's like a little church service."

"Oh, that's nice," I said.

Inwardly, I was thinking: *Church? Why would I want to go to church?* I had grown up in a home where the only times our parents took us to church was on Christmas and Easter. I knew Mom got mad at God when her father died at fifty-three years of age. She blamed Him for her father's cancer.

But Mickey . . . something was different about him. Maybe it was the way he looked me in the eye with a self-assurance of who he was and where he was going in life. Maybe it was because he wasn't full of himself. He was outgoing and interested in *me* as well as others. As nice a guy as he was, however, I never took Mickey up on Baseball Chapel while we were in Little Falls.

Then we were both promoted to the Columbia Mets. Since we knew each other in upstate New York, we naturally hung out a lot together. I realized that I didn't have to drink a lot of beer after the game to have fun. Mickey could hang out with us and tell stories and be the life of the party without getting blitzed.

Mickey kept inviting me to Baseball Chapel in Columbia. I kept making excuses . . . *I'm not ready . . . It's not my thing . . . maybe some other time.* At the same time, though, he was planting seeds in me—a desire to know who God was and how His Son Jesus Christ wanted to have a personal relationship with me.

A month into the season, I was languishing on the bench. Truth be told, I felt like I was spinning my wheels. Mickey asked if I wanted to come to Baseball Chapel. Instead of finding an excuse, I said yes to Mickey's invitation because I wanted what he had—an inner peace and serenity.

The pastor speaking that day shared the Gospel, explaining that we are all sinners, but that Jesus Christ went to the Cross and died for our sins so that we could have eternal life with Him. All we had to do to accept his free gift of salvation was to say "yes" to Jesus.

I knew I was a sinner. I knew I needed a Savior. That day, in the stillness of my heart, I took a step of faith. I knew I had a lot to learn about God, but I was willing to start the journey.

And what a journey it's been.

If you're a high school player, I invite you to check out the Fellowship of Christian Athletes or Athletes in Action. Find a good Bible-teaching church with contemporary music. Join a Bible study comprised of fellow baseball players. Another avenue is to check out Unlimited Potential (www.upi.org), a ministry that uses baseball to share the Good News in the U.S. and around the world. Mickey Weston is the international director.

It takes a special young person to make a decision for Christ and live for Him as a baseball or softball player. If you're on a faith journey, the best advice I can give you is to ask yourself, *How did I get here?*

You got here because God, through His Son, Jesus Christ, created you and gives you unique gifts needed to be part of a team of believers. If you keep that "swing thought" in mind, you'll be the best you can be—in life and on the baseball field.

So let me finish with this:

Jesus is real. He loves you, and He's waiting for you to ask Him into your heart. There's nothing we can do other than to accept His grace.

May God bless you all.

ABOUT THE AUTHORS

 STEVE SPRINGER is a former major league baseball player who spent eleven years at the Triple-A level, collecting 1,283 hits in 4,695 at-bats for a batting average of .269. He also reached the major leagues on two separate occasions in 1990 and 1992 with the Cleveland Indians and New York Mets, respectively. He played sparingly in the big leagues, going to bat 17 times and getting two hits in each league.

Steve moved into scouting following retirement and scouted for the Arizona Diamondbacks for five years and then became a baseball agent. One day, he recorded a CD on the mental side of hitting to give to his clients. His homey-yet-direct talk was so well-received that college and high school baseball coaches asked him to address their teams, which led to more speaking requests. In addition to his speaking career, Steve was hired as a "performance coach" with the Toronto Blue Jays in 2008, working mainly with their minor league teams.

As demand grew for his insights on hitting, Steve started Quality at-Bats. He produced DVDs and CDs on his philosophy of hitting that sold like proverbial hotcakes, traveled around the country speaking before baseball audiences, and made himself available for private hitting lessons known as "Spend the Day with Spring." He also launched subscription-based online baseball academy, where young ballplayers can upload video of their swings for critiquing by Steve. Subscribers can also watch videos of a 12-year-old and an 18-year-old batter receiving instruction on how to better hit a baseball as well as improve their mental approach to hitting. For more information on the Quality at-Bats Academy, please visit www.qualityatbatsacademy.com.

Steve and his wife, Teri, are the parents of two adult children, Cody and Logan, and make their home in Huntington Beach, California.

For more information on Steve Springer and tips on becoming a better player, please visit his main website at www.qualityatbats.com.

 **MIKE YORKEY** is the author or co-author of more than one hundred books with more than 2 million copies in print. His latest book is *After the Cheering Stops* with Cyndy Feasel, who tells Cyndy's tragic story of her family's journey into chaos and darkness resulting from the damage her husband, Grant Feasel of the Seattle Seahawks, suffered due to football-related concussions and head trauma.

Mike has also collaborated with the Chicago Cubs' Ben Zobrist and his wife, Julianna, a Christian music artist, in *Double Play*; San Francisco Giants pitcher Dave Dravecky in *Called Up*; Washington Redskins quarterback Colt McCoy and his father, Brad, in *Growing Up Colt*; San Diego Chargers placekicker Rolf Benirschke in *Alive & Kicking*; tennis star Michael Chang in *Holding Serve*; and paralyzed Rutgers' defensive tackle Eric LeGrand in *Believe: My Faith and the Tackle That Changed My Life*. Mike is also the co-author of the internationally bestselling *Every Man's Battle* series with Steve Arterburn and Fred Stoeker.

He and his wife, Nicole, are the parents of two adult children and make their home in Encinitas, California.

Mike's website is www.mikeyorkey.com.

INVITE STEVE SPRINGER TO SPEAK TODAY

Steve Springer is an entertaining as well as dynamic speaker on the topic of hitting, baseball, and the analogy of baseball and sales in business. He speaks regularly around the country and also leads clinics for a variety of teams at the college, high school, and Little League levels.

If you, your team, or your business would like Steve to come speak at your event, please visit his website at www.qualityatbats.com and click on the Contact button. Steve is also available for private mentoring.

CHECK OUT STEVE SPRINGER'S QUALITY AT-BAT LINEUP CARDS, SCOREBOOKS, AND HELMET STICKERS

With the 2017 season, Steve Springer is now offering Quality at-Bat Lineup Cards and Scorebooks that coaches and parents can use to encourage their youngsters to have a quality at-bat rather than putting all their focus on getting a base hit. Little League and youth baseball players will also love being awarded colorful Quality at-Bat helmet stickers for every quality at-bat.

For more information on Steve's Quality at-Bat Lineup Cards, Scorebooks, and Helmet Stickers, please visit www.qualityatbats.com.